GreatCentsBooks

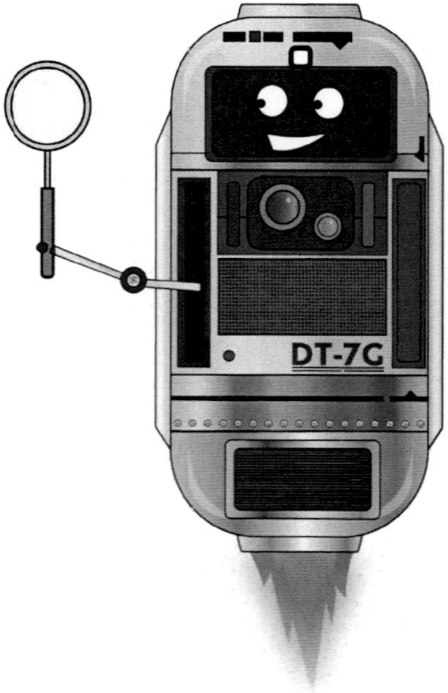

For permission requests, please contact:
GreatCents Books
bteich@greatcents.org

Edited by: Blake Teichmeier

Junior Editor: Augustine Hanson

This book is a work of nonfiction. Any resemblance to actual persons, living or dead, is purely coincidental.

Printed in the United States of America.

ISBN: 978-1-971213-03-3

First Edition: December 2024
Printed in the United States of America

To my son Arthur & my grandparents
May wisdom always guide you,
whether young or old.

This book is part of the series called **Galactic Growth**. Our goal is to help you think about your **mind & money.**

Who are you dedicating your work on this book to:

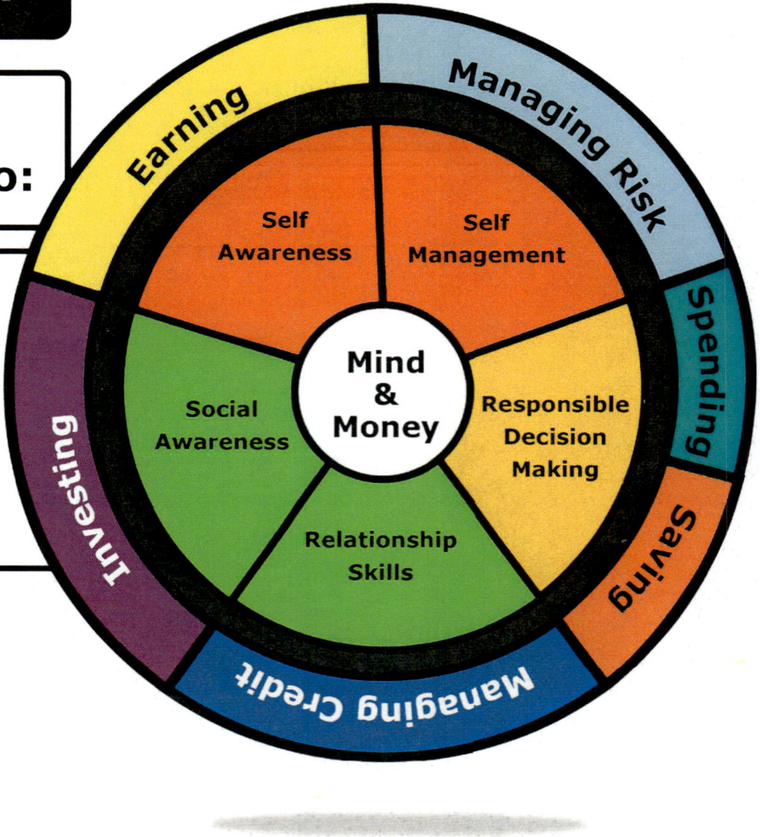

Table of Contents

This book belongs to:

Galactic Growth!

Social Emotional Learning & Personal Finances

Better Start Budgeting!

Written and Illustrated by:
Blake Teichmeier

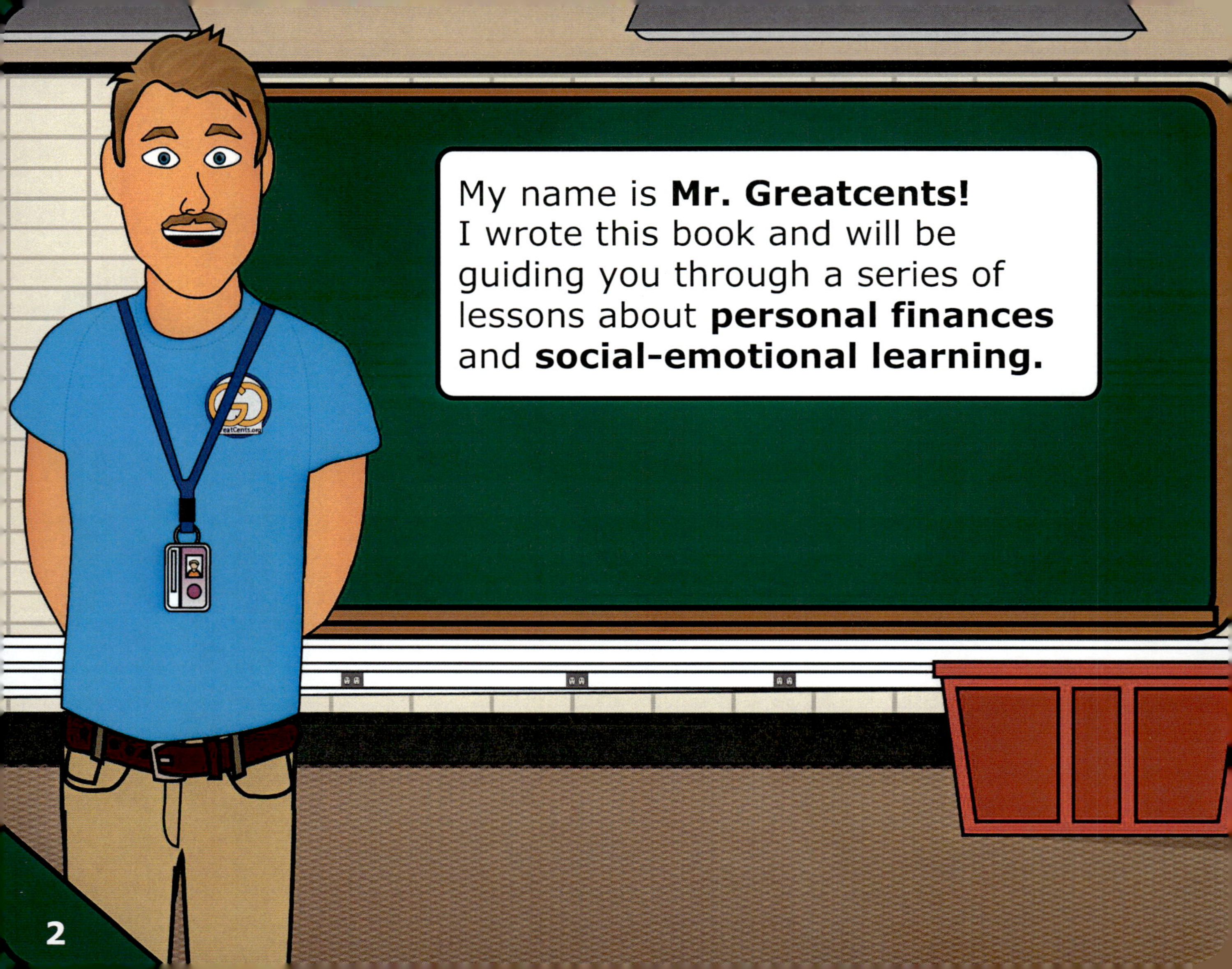
My name is **Mr. Greatcents!** I wrote this book and will be guiding you through a series of lessons about **personal finances** and **social-emotional learning.**
GreatCents.org

You are getting older, and with that comes **new responsibilities**. You will need to be more aware of your **mind**, the choices you make, and your **money**, and the way you spend and save your money. Join me as we leave our familiar world behind and venture into a universe of learning!

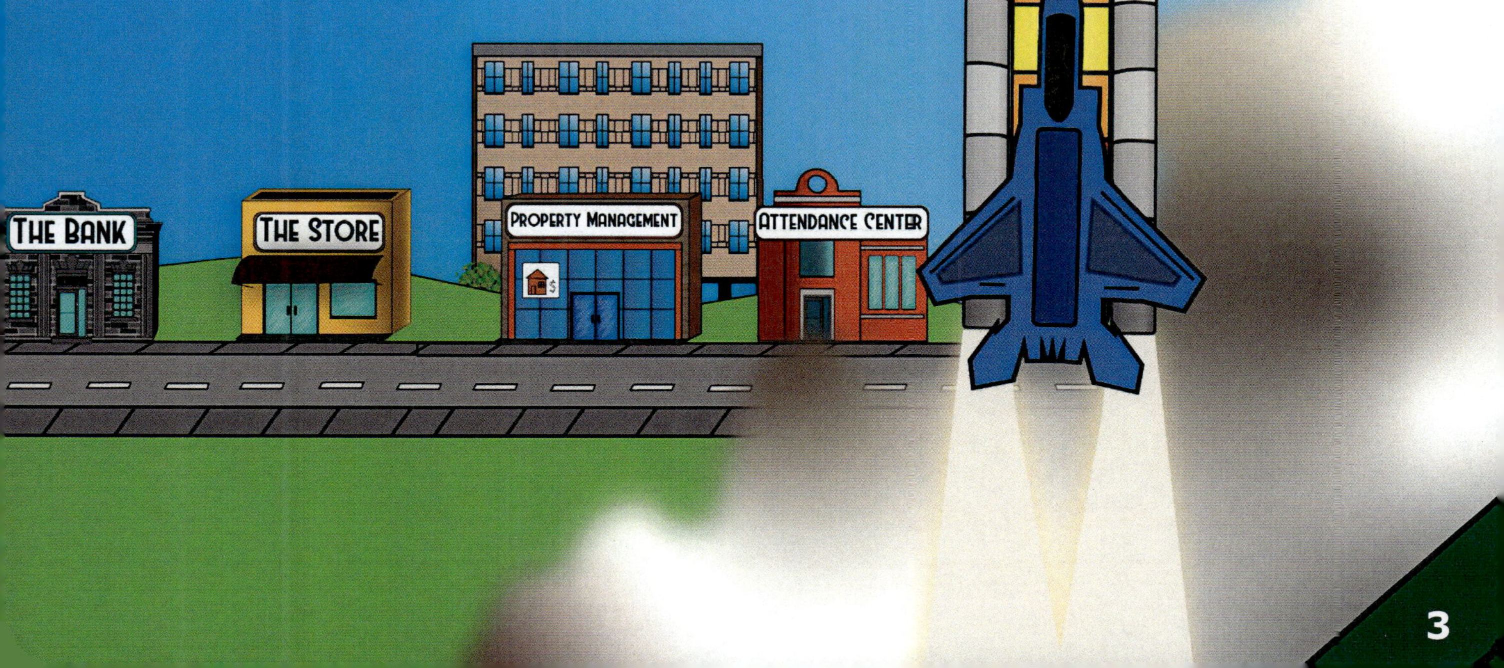

When you are faced with a choice how do you make your decision?
DT-7G
This is my robot DT-7G, he is going to help us on our journey

Galactic Growth!

Social Emotional Learning & Personal Finances

Better Start Budgeting!

Our Goal:
Make responsible decisions for our **personal** and **financial** lives.

Step 1:
Identify the steps in making responsible decisions.

Step 2:
Observe how budgeting is a way to be financially responsible.

Step 3:
Recognize the different parts of a budget and the power of saving.

Step 4:
Create a budget for your current life and for the future.

Everyday is filled with thousands of choices! Many of which you don't even realize you are making. That is why you have to be **intentional**, meaning you put thought into it.

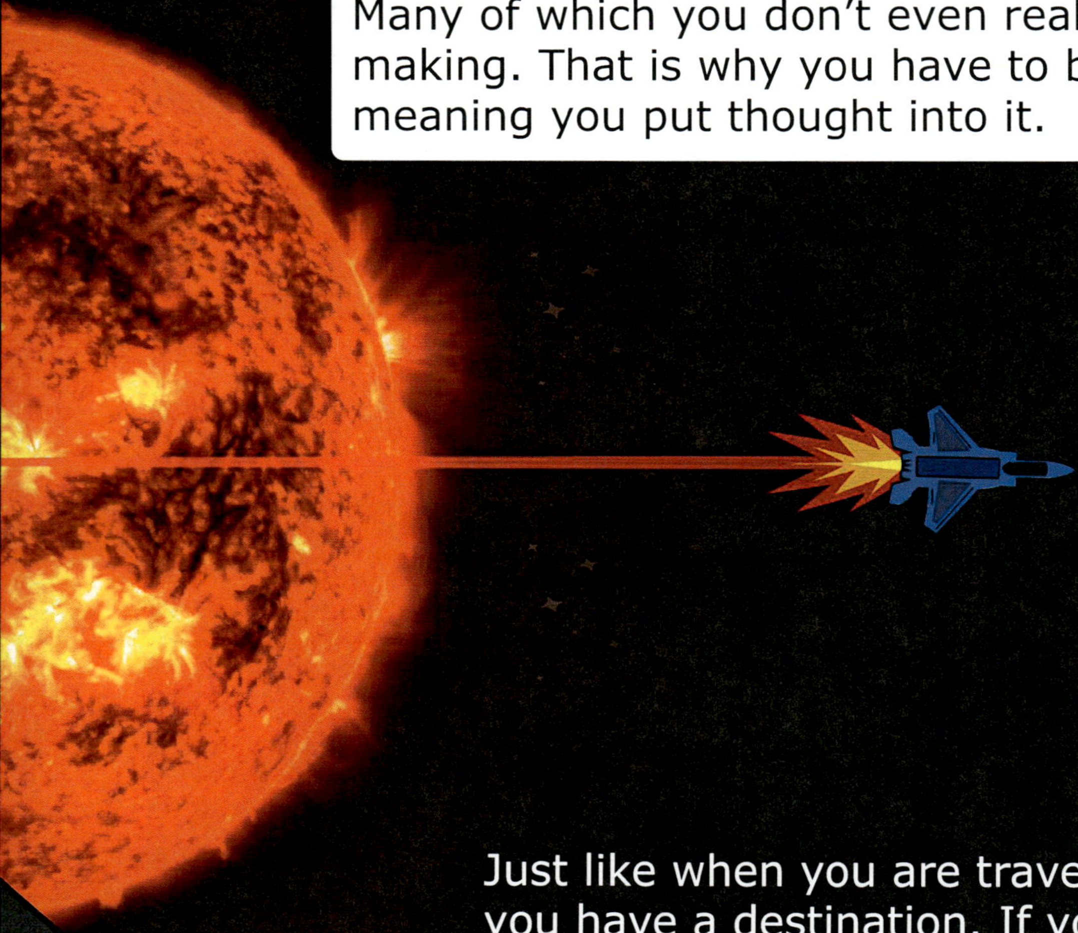

Just like when you are traveling somewhere you have a destination. If you don't make the right turns you could end up lost!

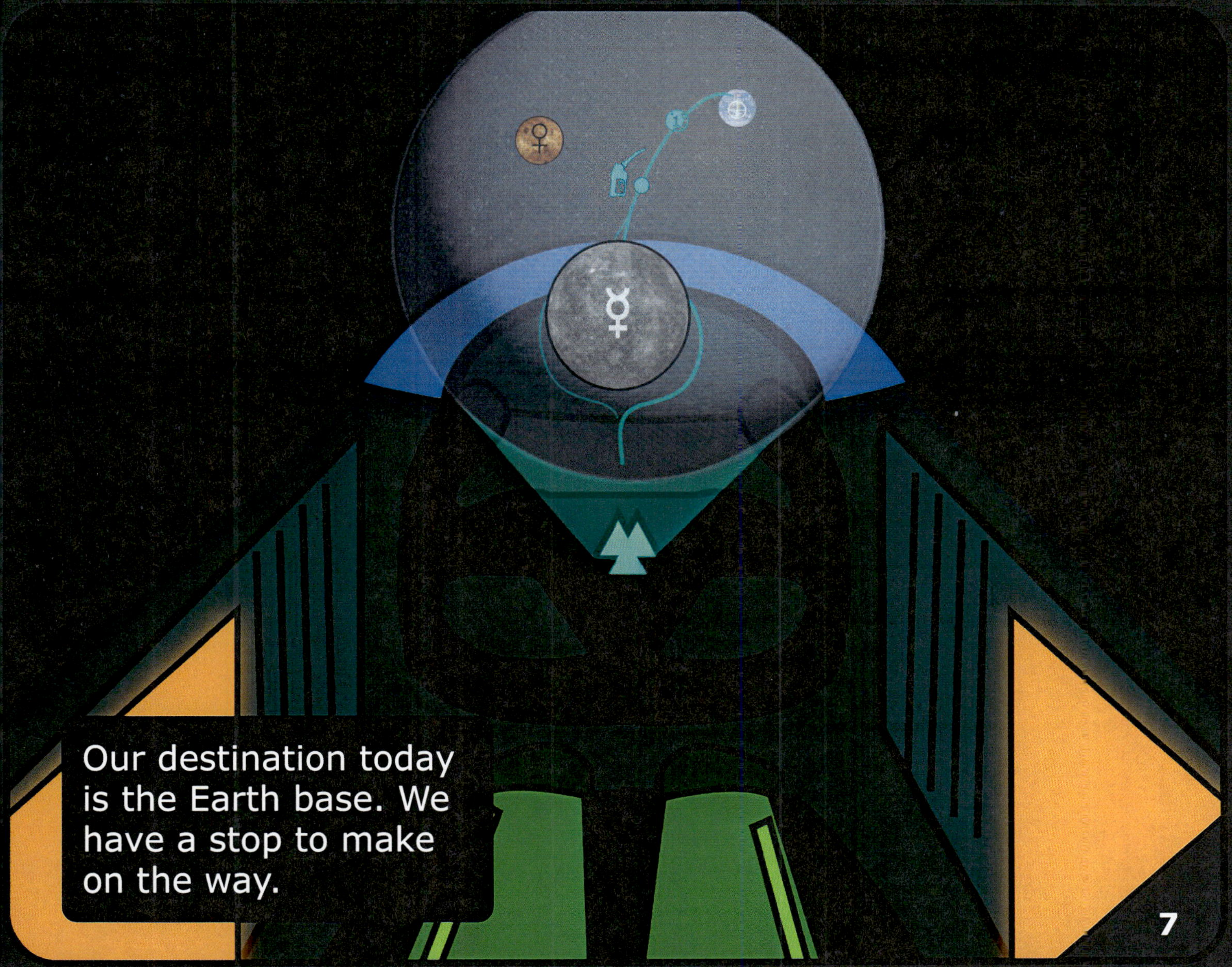
Our destination today is the Earth base. We have a stop to make on the way.

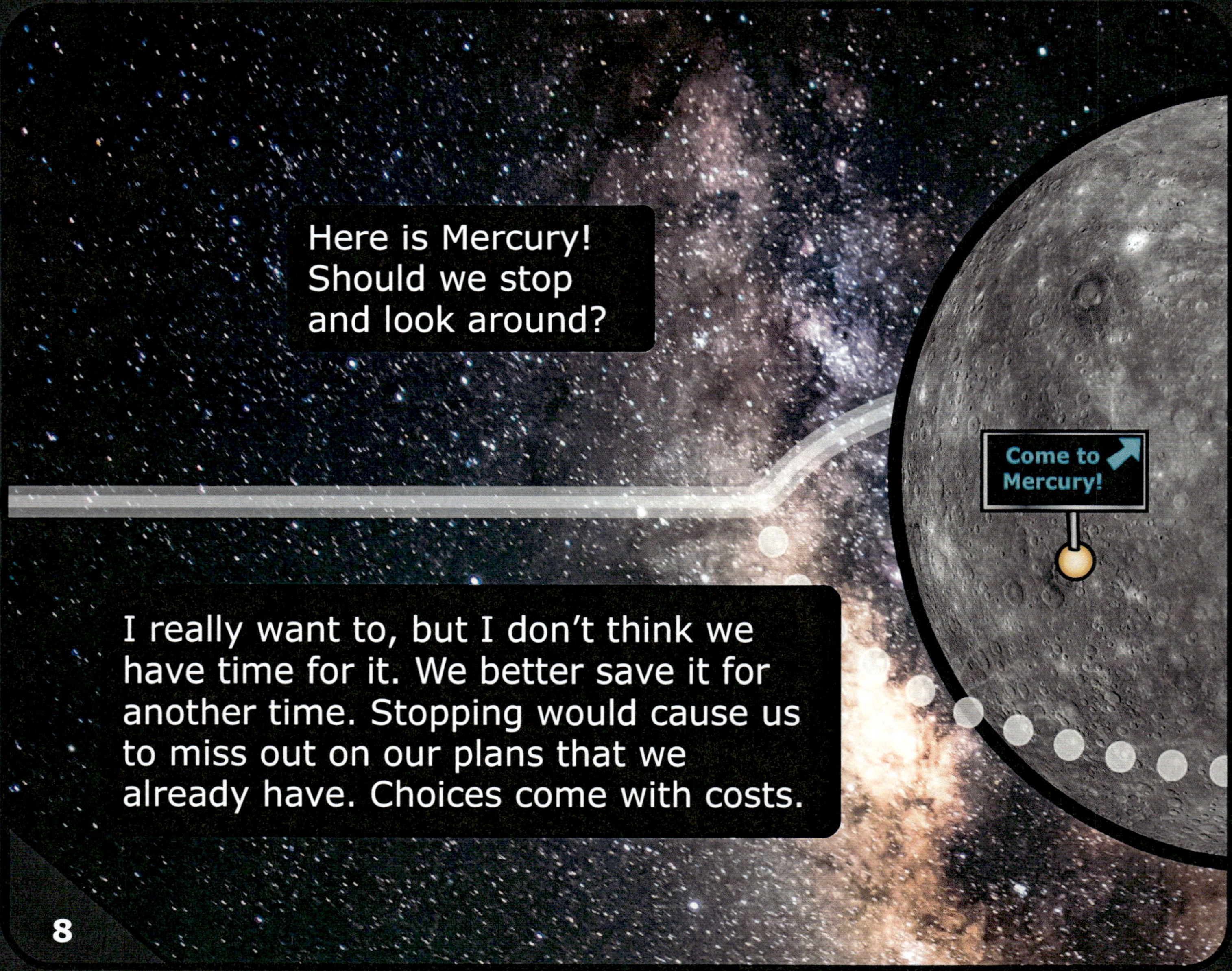
Here is Mercury! Should we stop and look around?
Come to Mercury!
I really want to, but I don't think we have time for it. We better save it for another time. Stopping would cause us to miss out on our plans that we already have. Choices come with costs.

Making choices is a skill! We call this responsible decision making!

Responsible Decision-Making:
Recognizing the factors involved in making a choice and considering how those choices will affect the future.

Key Word

How do you make responsible decisions? We are going to look at 4 keys parts!

Priorities→ **Options→** **Costs→** **Results→**

What are your priorities?

Priority:
Something that is more important than others.

Review

In our first adventure, the book *Mind & Money* we talked about priorities.
To make good decisions you need to be clear about what is important to you.
Then you must ask yourself, **"does this choice support my priorities?"**

Two things you really need to prioritize is your **Mind & Money**. How you interact with yourself and others and how you manage your money will have a huge impact on your overall well being.

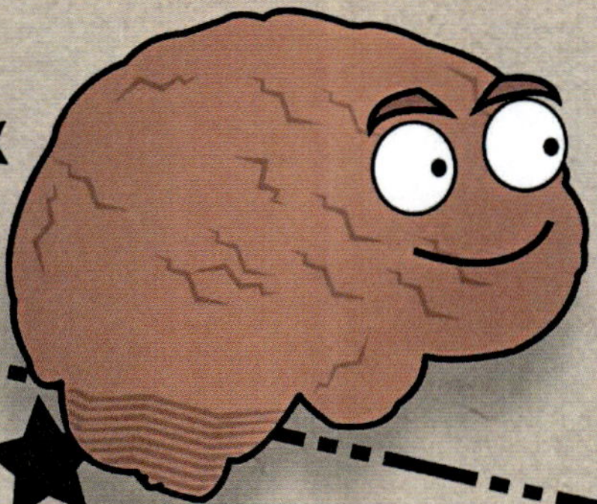

Making good choices about your mind include: self awareness, self management, social awareness, relationships skills and responsible decision making.

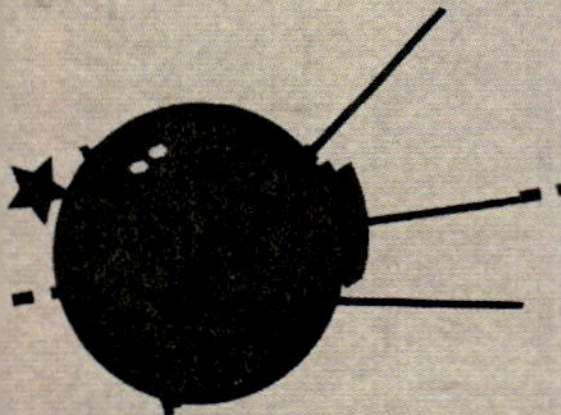

Making good choices about your money include: earning, spending, saving, investing, credit and handling risk.

Priorities?

Throughout your life, you'll develop the skill of distinguishing between wants and needs. Check out these examples!

Bread can keep you alive, **it's a need, something essential to survive.**
What else do you need to survive?

Cake is tasty, but you don't need it to live. **It's a want, something you'd like, but can live without.**
What are other things like that?

Needs come first. We prioritize what's most important. When faced with a choice, ask yourself: Is this bread or cake?

This same idea of prioritizing applies to our goals. There are millions of things you could do, but what will you have the time, energy, and resources to actually do?

What are your top 2 priorities at school?

1.

2.

What are your top 2 priorities at home?

1.

2.

What are your top 2 money priorities?

1.

2.

What are your options?

Good thing we didn't stop at Mercury, we are running low on gas.

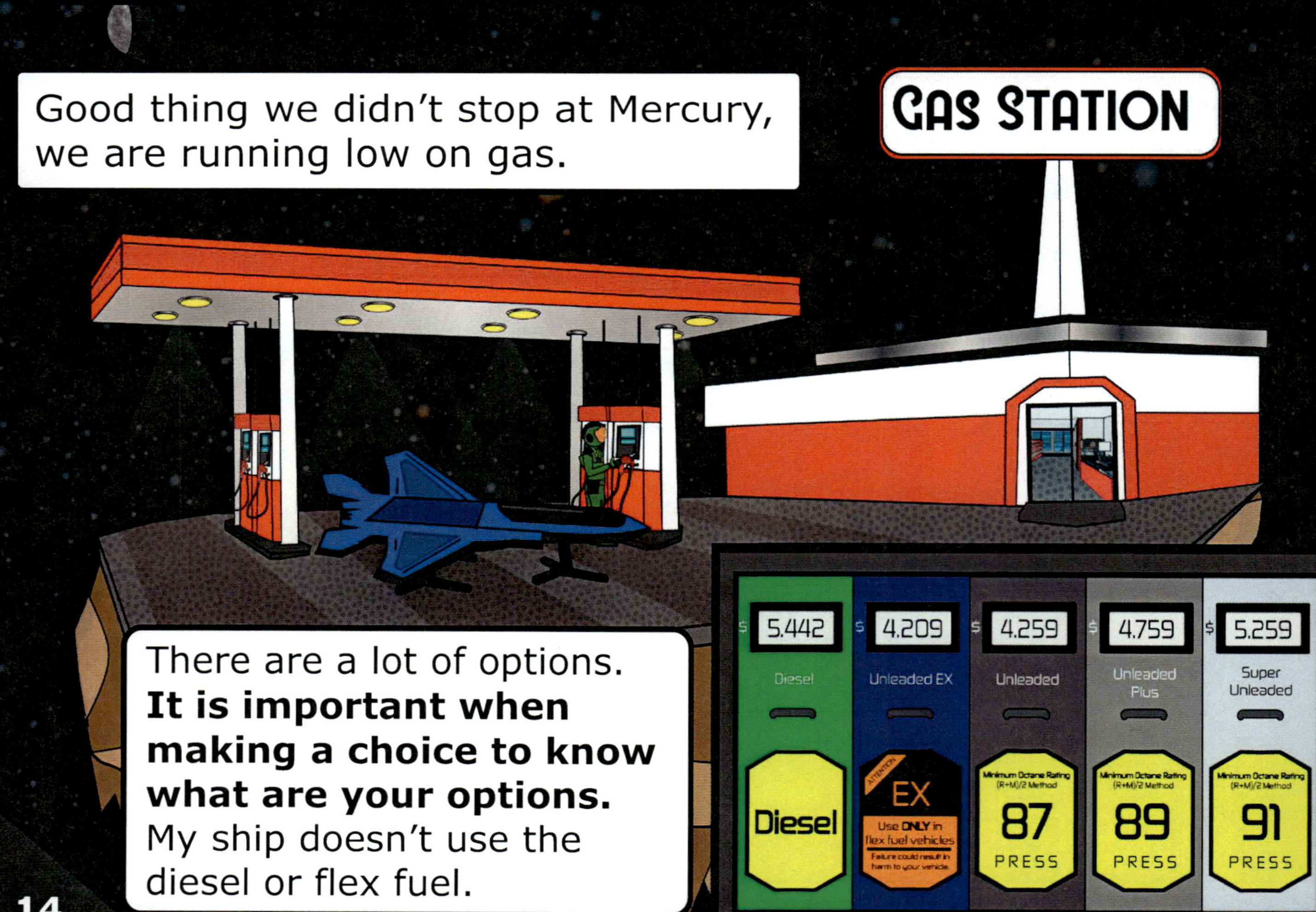

There are a lot of options. **It is important when making a choice to know what are your options.** My ship doesn't use the diesel or flex fuel.

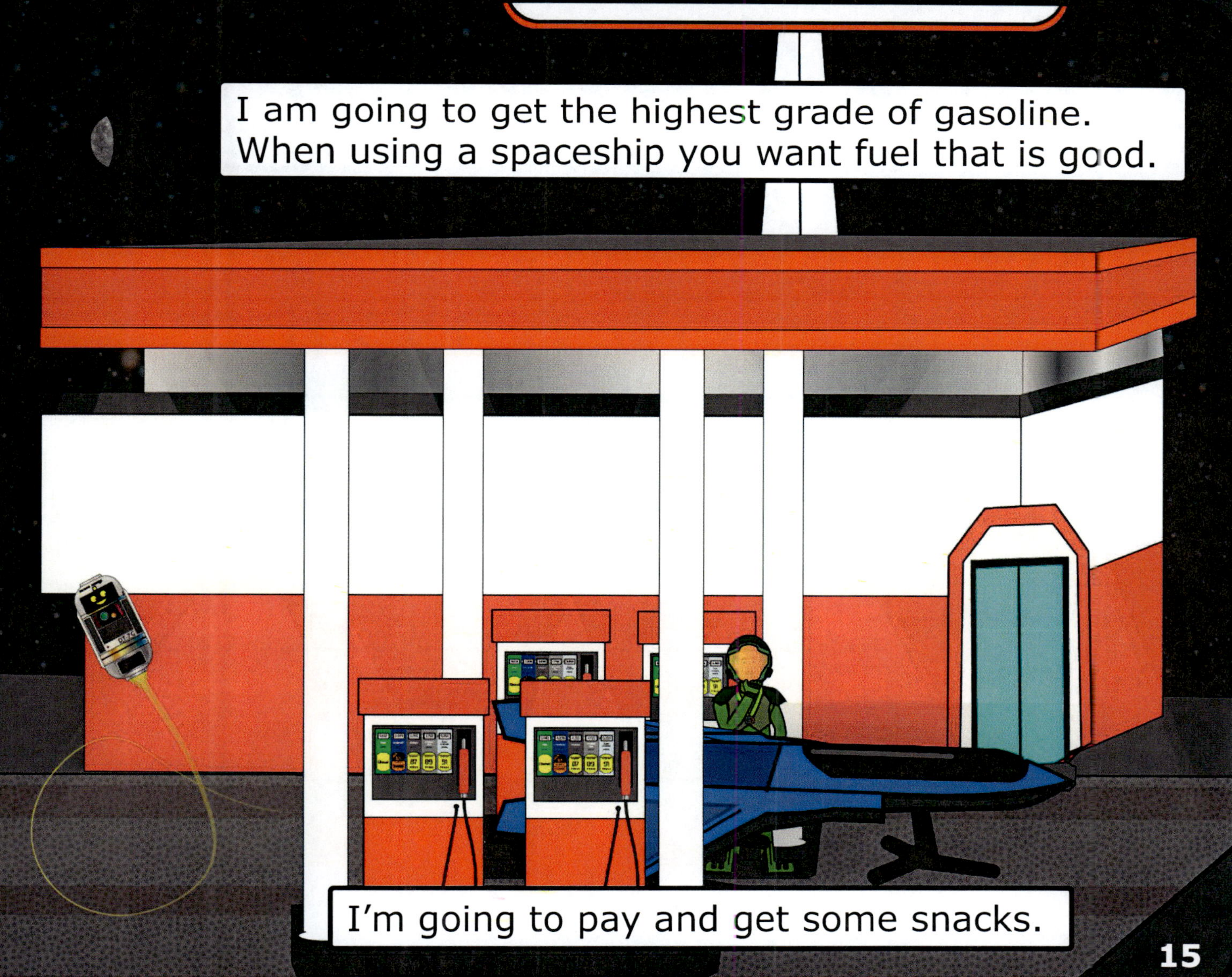
I am going to get the highest grade of gasoline. When using a spaceship you want fuel that is good.
I'm going to pay and get some snacks.

Options?

"Where do you want to eat?"
It's a question friends ask all the time.
Life is full of options and choices!

What are your three favorite restaurants? Why?

1.

2.

3.

Step 1: Choose a restaurant you enjoy or imagine your own.				
Step 2: List 12 items from the menu along with their prices.				
Step 3: Select two items from your list and draw them.				

What are choices you have already made? Remember!

Morning	Afternoon
What did you eat for breakfast yesterday, and what other choices did you have? What did you wear yesterday?	What did you eat for lunch yesterday, and what were your other options? Did you spend this time learning, relaxing, or doing something fun?

Evening	Night
Did you spend time with anyone yesterday evening? What did you do? Draw a picture!	What time did you go to bed last night? What is your nighttime routine? (What you do before you go to sleep)

What are the costs?

Everything you do takes time and often requires money. This means you need to think about what you have before committing to something or making a purchase. Do you have enough money? Time? Energy?

If you want to take decision making to the next level you want to consider what is your opportunity cost!

Opportunity Cost:
What a person gives up when making a choice.

Key Word

Sadly, I don't have enough money to get a hotdog. That is the cost of getting the more expensive gas and that is okay. If you could only pick one thing from the gas station what would it be? What would be your second choice?
1st Choice:
2nd Choice:
Connie

Costs?

Take a moment to recognize the parts of a choice:

Story about a choice:	Their Choice:	Opportunity Cost:
Ex. Michael was deciding between buying a new pair of shoes or a new game. He chose the game.	**Ex.** He bought the new game.	**Ex.** The new pair of shoes he didn't purchase.
Maria was invited to go to the movies with a friend but had a lot of homework. She chose to stay home.		
Now, come up with your own example!		

Before making a choice, it's important to count the cost.
This means considering how your decision will affect your life.

Time!

Money!

Energy!

"Can this fit into my schedule? How?"
Life can get busy, so it's important to keep track of your plans. **How do you keep track of your schedule?**

"How much will this cost? For how long?"
Money is a scarce resource, meaning there's only so much of it. **How do you track your spending?**

"Will I have the energy to do this?"
Our attitude and productivity are greatly influenced by our energy levels.
What is an activity that gives you energy?

What are the results?

Everything around you is the result of choices that were made.

Consider the clothes you are wearing right now. They exist because someone made the choice to show up to work. Then through a long process of shipping and selling they found their way to you. Then you made the choice to wear them today. You are wearing the results!

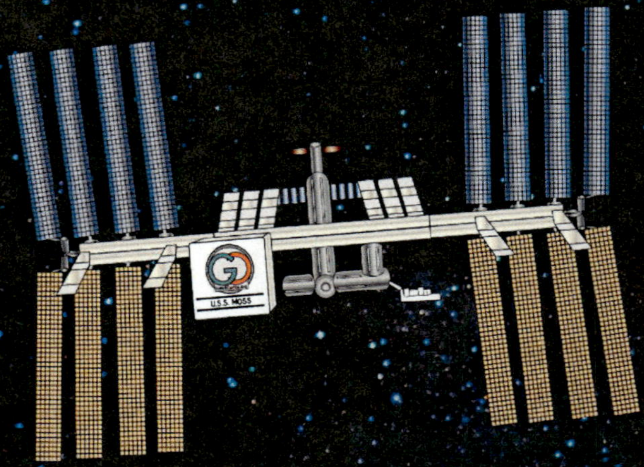

When making choices you need to **reflect on outcomes. Even better is when you can watch others and study their results.** Learn the power of understanding cause and effect!

Cause and Effect:
When one thing happens (**the cause**), it leads to something else happening (**the effect**).

Key Word

Who is someone older that you can watch and learn from?

Person:

Results?

Thinking ahead is a valuable skill known as anticipation. It can save you time, money, energy, and help you avoid potential problems.

Let's practice this skill by anticipating what could likely happen!

Cause	Effect
Cause: You studied really hard for your test.	Effect:
Cause: You forgot to set your alarm last night.	Effect:
Cause: You saved $5 of your weekly allowance.	Effect:
Cause: You helped a classmate with a math problem.	Effect:
Cause: You left your bike outside during a rainstorm.	Effect:
Cause: You borrowed $50 from you friend.	Effect:

You might think this sounds like a lot of work and it is. However, if you give it a try you will find that it helps you to make decisions you are proud of!

Choices take time!

Priorities	Options
Mind: What are somethings you do to take care of yourself? **Money:** What are somethings you do to be financially responsible?	**Avoid impulse choices.** This means making a choice before thinking about all your options. **Describe a choice that could be made quickly?** **What is an example of a choice you should take time to make?**
Costs	**Results**
"What am I giving up?" We want to feel confident that our choice was worth whatever we were giving up. **Money:** Can you afford this choice? **Time:** Will this conflict with things you are already doing? **Energy:** Can you still be a good version of yourself while doing this? **Opportunities:** How will this shape your future choices?	**Not all results happen right away.** Sometimes, the best choices don't feel good at the moment, but they lead to great things later. This is called delayed gratification. **Share a choice you could make today that might be tough now. Would that choice help you out later?**

Let's apply this to some of your decision making!

What is a choice you made recently?	
How does this align with your priorities?	
What were your options when making this choice?	
What did you give up when making this choice? (Time, money, energy?)	
Are you happy with the results of your choice? How come?	

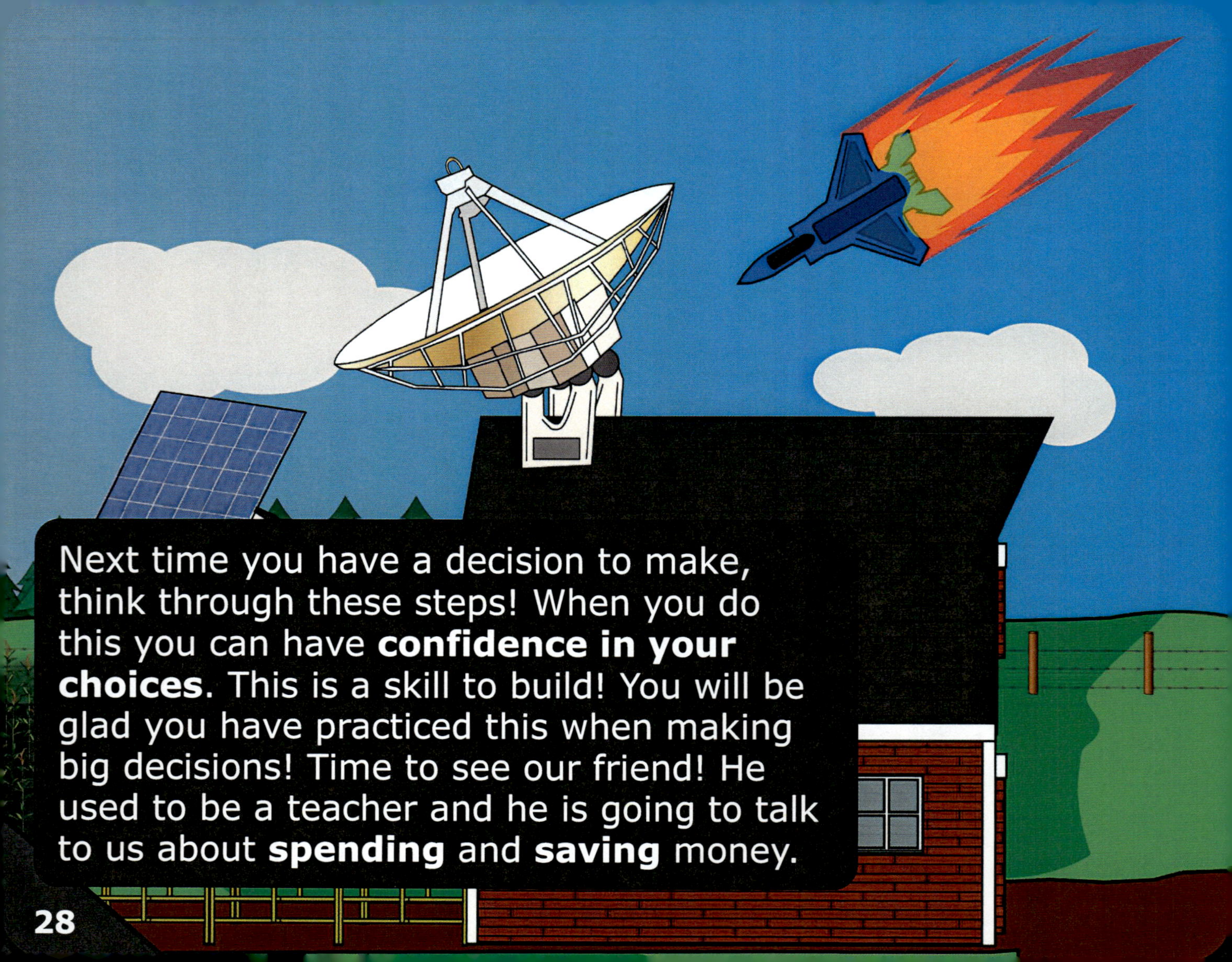

Next time you have a decision to make, think through these steps! When you do this you can have **confidence in your choices**. This is a skill to build! You will be glad you have practiced this when making big decisions! Time to see our friend! He used to be a teacher and he is going to talk to us about **spending** and **saving** money.

Beep-Beep!

Examine two choices you made today!

Choice:	Options:	Costs:	Results:

Step 1:
Identify the steps in making responsible decisions.

1

You have power in the choices you make! Every day, you are shaping your tomorrow. Think about your options, weigh the costs, and make your choices!

DT7G, we're not in Space anymore...
Beeeeeeep... Beep.
We have arrived at the farm! A tad bit smelly and dirty, but **there is lots to learn here!**
DT-7G

THE FARM
Welcome everyone! **My name is Mr. T.** Back in the day, I was both a farmer and a teacher. Today, we're going to talk about **how you can manage your money.** Come back to the office!

As a farmer, you face many choices: what to grow, how much seed to plant, how much fertilizer to use, how to handle bugs, when to harvest, and how much to keep or sell.
GARDEN SEEDS
Plant it in the soil and watch it grow!
Having a plan is crucial! Without one, you can run into all kinds of problems. **What fruits or veggies would you like to grow?**

As a teacher, you make a lot of choices. What topic are you teaching? What are the students learning? How long will it take? Who are your students? What do they already know? And how will you know they've learned it?

The more you know, the better choices you can usually make. **What's your favorite thing to learn about?**

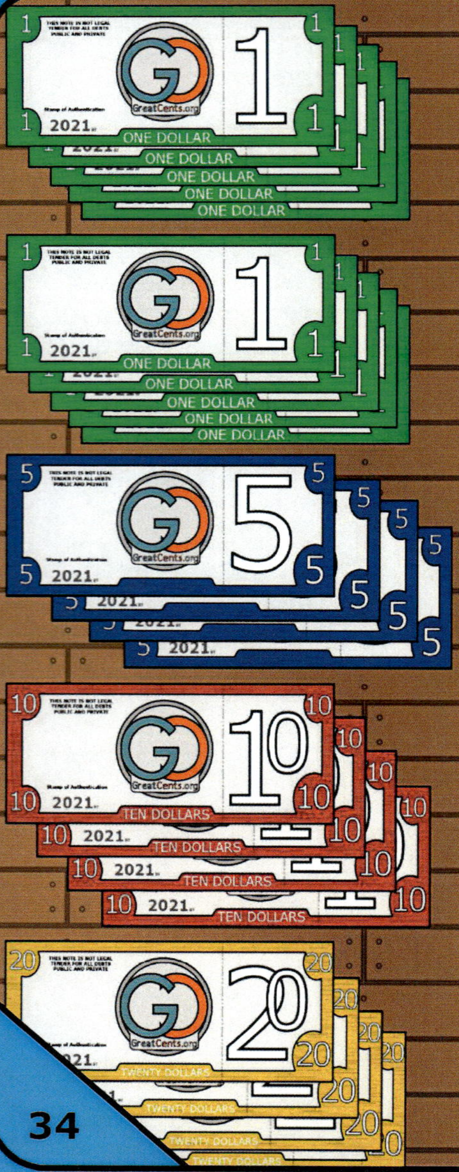

I'm giving you $150. Your task is to make a plan for how you're going to use it. You have 100% freedom! Spend, save, give—it's up to you. Write your plan on the next page!

You have $150—now it's your turn to decide what to do with it! Will you spend it, save it, give some away, or do a mix of all three? **Write your plan below. Be specific!**

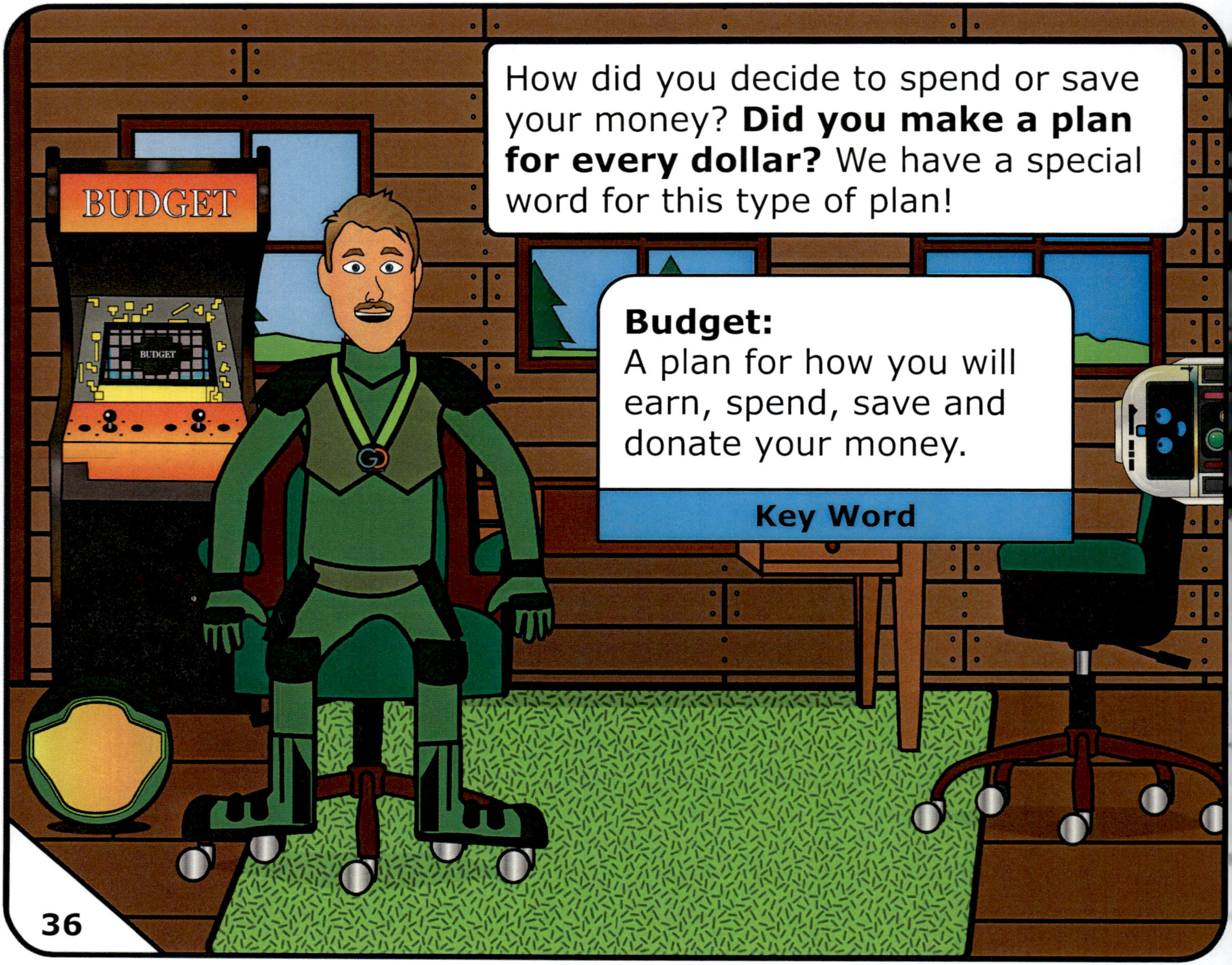
BUDGET
BUDGET
How did you decide to spend or save your money? **Did you make a plan for every dollar?** We have a special word for this type of plan!
Budget:
A plan for how you will earn, spend, save and donate your money.
Key Word

Let's take a moment to learn some lessons from the farm. Sometimes it helps to learn something through a story. **Listen to this tale of two sisters!**

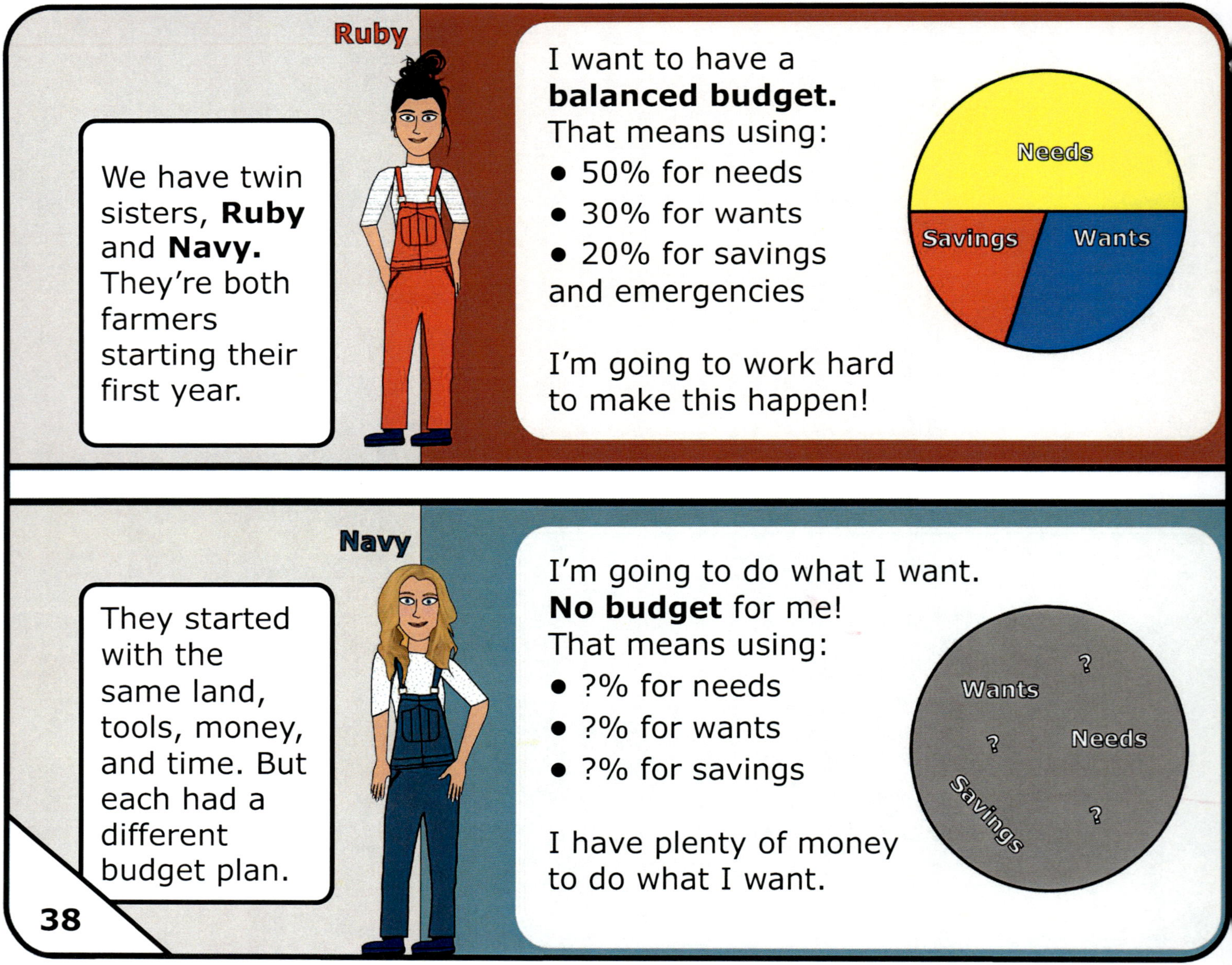
Ruby
We have twin sisters, **Ruby** and **Navy.** They're both farmers starting their first year.
I want to have a **balanced budget.** That means using:
• 50% for needs
• 30% for wants
• 20% for savings and emergencies
I'm going to work hard to make this happen!
Needs
Savings
Wants
Navy
They started with the same land, tools, money, and time. But each had a different budget plan.
I'm going to do what I want. **No budget** for me! That means using:
• ?% for needs
• ?% for wants
• ?% for savings
I have plenty of money to do what I want.
Wants
?
?
Needs
Savings
?

Budget

How does a person make a budget?

Step 1:
Make Money

• Find a way you can earn some money, if possible a way you can do on a regular basis.

For example, mowing a neighbor's lawn or babysitting.

What could you do to make money?

Would this be a one time thing or could you do this regularly?

How much would you make?

Step 2:
Safe Space

• You need a place you can put you cash so you won't have to worry about it.

First, you will want a wallet or purse to carry your money on you.

Second, you will want a bank account you can put larger amounts of money in.

Do you have a wallet or purse?
If yes, what does it look like?

If no, Where could you get one?

Where could you get a bank account?

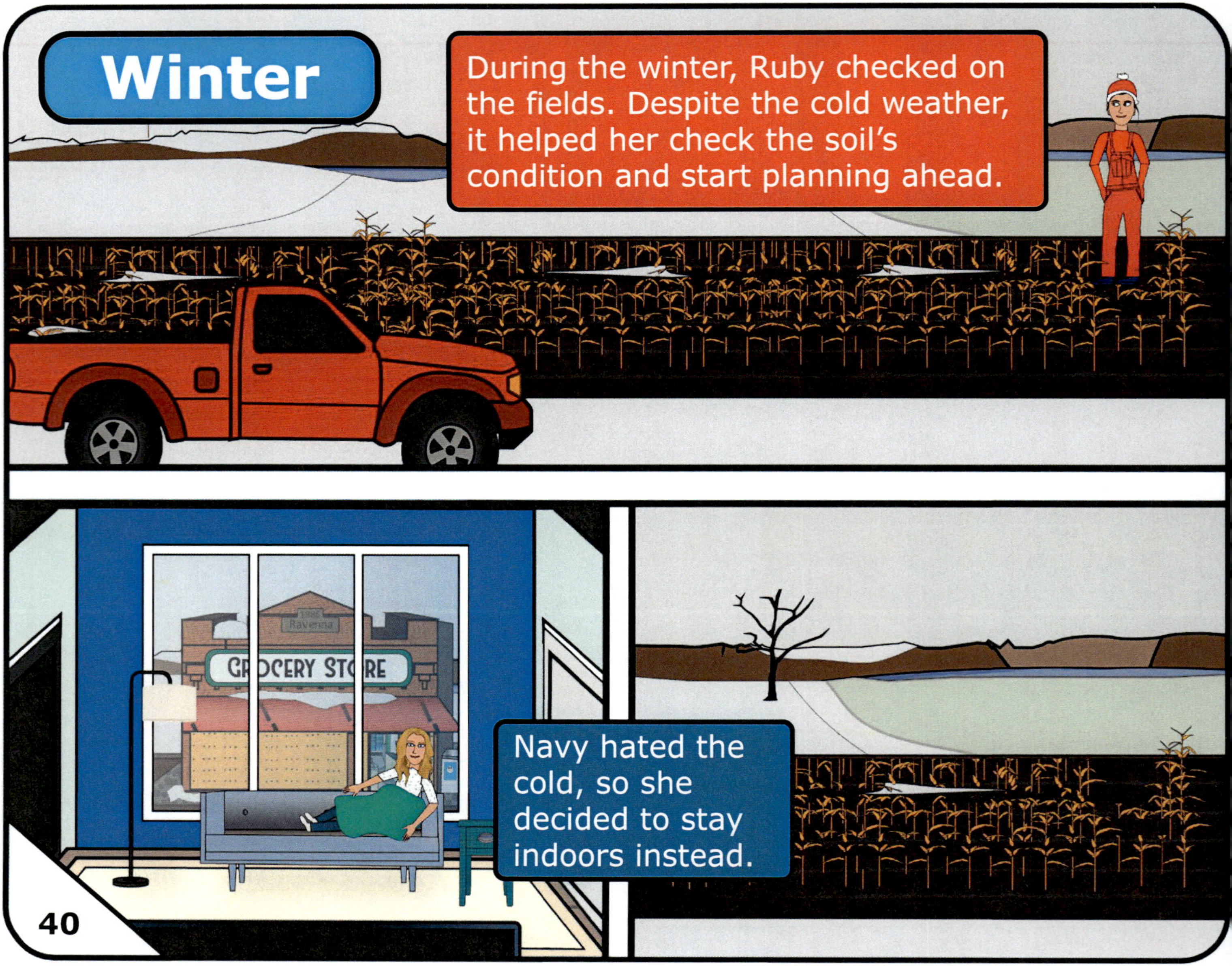
Winter
During the winter, Ruby checked on the fields. Despite the cold weather, it helped her check the soil's condition and start planning ahead.
Ravenna
GROCERY STORE
Navy hated the cold, so she decided to stay indoors instead.

Planning

Are you a planner? For some people this comes more natural. Others need to push themselves!

A plan is like a blueprint, how will you build your spending? A strong budget prioritizes needs, makes room for wants and thinks about the future!

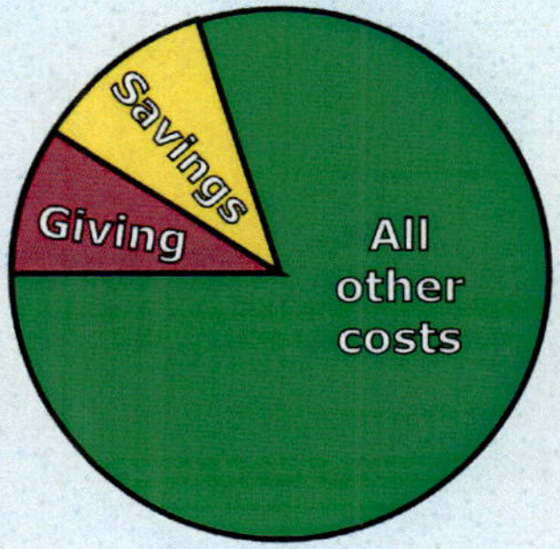

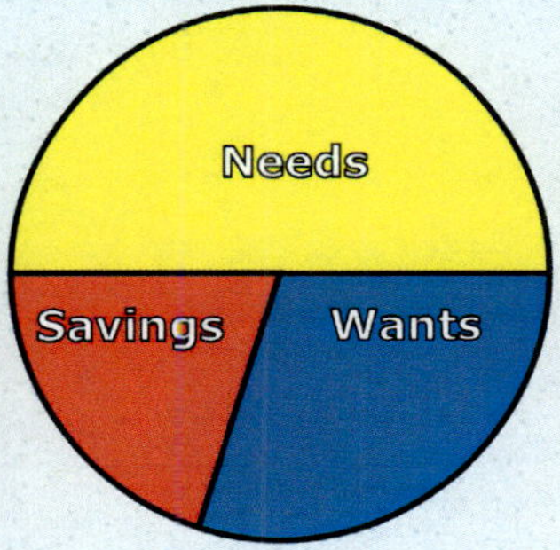

Step 3:
Make a Plan

• Write it down! We are much more likely to do things that are recorded somewhere. You could do this on a piece of paper, a notebook or online.

Where could you write down your budget?

Percentages are helpful!

• When you first get your money you will want to break it into sections. Putting your money in separate envelopes can also help to separate spending, saving and donating.

A simple plan is the **10-10-80.**

10% (Donate) 10% (Save) 80% (Other costs)

A another plan is the **20-30-50.**

50% (Needs) 30% (Wants) 20% (Savings)

How does having a budget help you to make responsible decisions?

Spring
Ruby chose to rent her grandpa's tractor, which was convenient since he lived nearby, and it saved her a lot of money.
I'd love a new tractor, but this one works just fine. I need seed, fertilizer, fuel, and a few other things. I'm glad I got insurance, you never know what could happen.
20
2021
GreatCents.org
50
100

Navy decided to buy a brand-new tractor, just because she really wanted one. She went to the bank and took out a loan to pay for it.
I'm going to get a new tractor and planter. It has all the cool technology, and I'll make payments each month.
I'm going to look so good in my new tractor!
NAVY
1988
Date: 3/28/24
Pay to the Order of: Turtle Tractors
$825
Eight Hundred and twenty five dollars
Dollars
Memo: Tractor
Navy
1:123456789I: 1:987654321I: 1988

Planting

**Having a plan gives you direction!
This means it will guide you as you spend!**

Step 4:
Practice

• When faced with a situation where you can spend money you will want to look back to your budget. It will likely make the decision for you!

• **Do you have the money for it in your budget?** If the answer is **no**, then you don't get it. If there is money the next questions is, **"is it worth it?"**

• Strategic spending is a skill and the more you do it the better you will get!

What is a need you have that you should budget for?

What is something you would like to budget for fun?

Summer
One day, a huge storm rolled through and damaged all the fields in the area.
Some of the corn was flattened by the wind, and other parts were damaged by hail.
Thankfully, Ruby had insurance, and she was told it would cover some of the damage. She had planned ahead in case something like this happened.
Navy didn't buy insurance. It was optional, and she chose to skip it. Now, she had to wait and see what the damage would cost her.

Persevering

Life is filled with unexpected moments! What will you do when they happen?

Step 5:

Keep at it

- Often goals seem easy at first, but as time goes on they get more difficult.
- **For example,** it can be hard to give up a want in order to keep your budget.
- You need to build **perseverance.** This means you keep working, even when it gets tough, knowing that it's worth it!

Tip: When things get hard remind yourself of your goals and how good it will feel to be responsible.

What is an unexpected cost that could make meeting your goals difficult?

How could you protect yourself from unexpected costs?

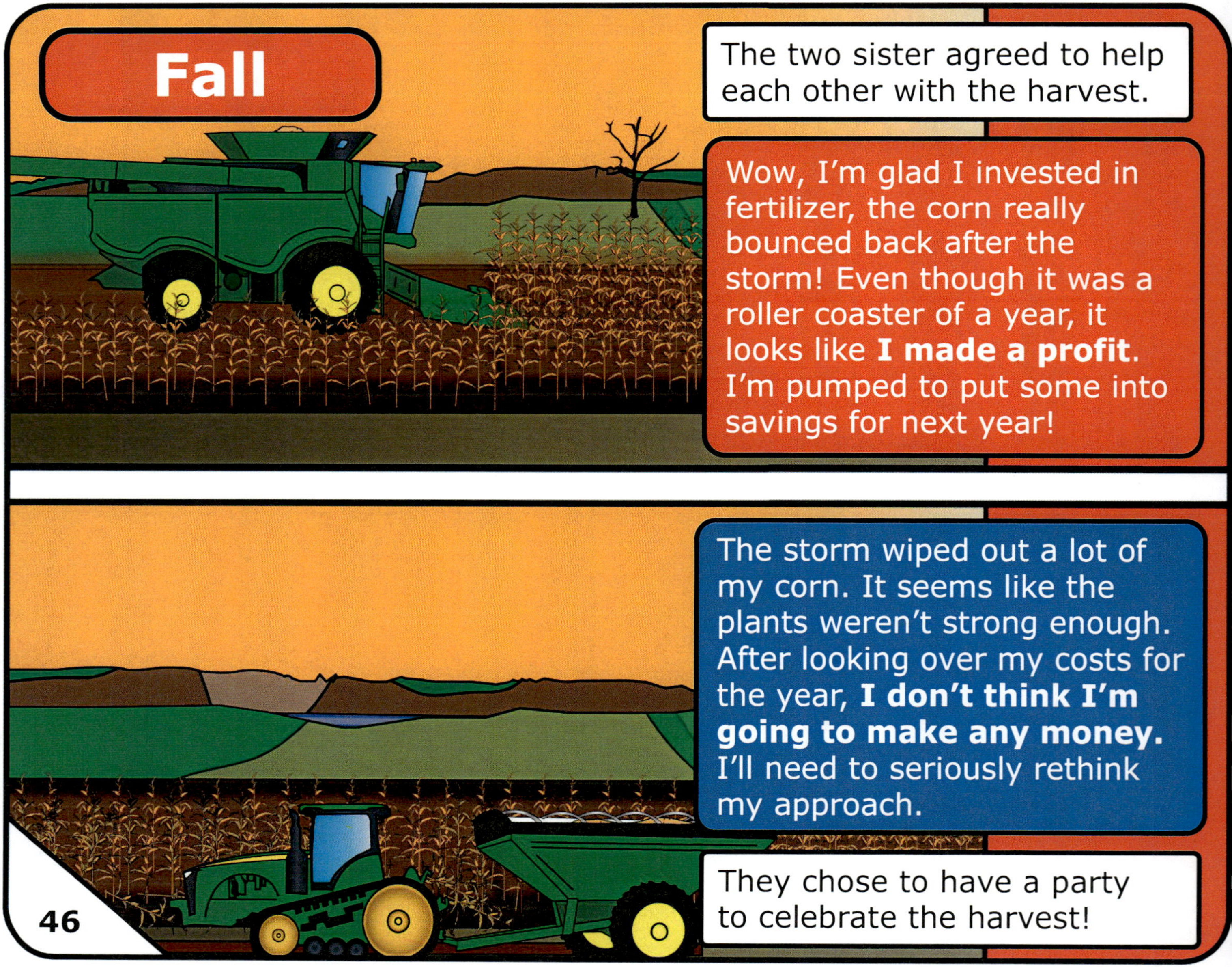
Fall
The two sister agreed to help each other with the harvest.
Wow, I'm glad I invested in fertilizer, the corn really bounced back after the storm! Even though it was a roller coaster of a year, it looks like **I made a profit**. I'm pumped to put some into savings for next year!
The storm wiped out a lot of my corn. It seems like the plants weren't strong enough. After looking over my costs for the year, **I don't think I'm going to make any money.** I'll need to seriously rethink my approach.
They chose to have a party to celebrate the harvest!

Harvesting

The cause and effect of a month of managing your money! Worth it?

Step 6:
Review

- As you manage your money your going to find that **you made mistakes** and that is okay. That is part of the process of budgeting!
- If a category needs more money, you can adjust the amount by taking from another category.
- If you find yourself overspending in ways you don't want, make a plan.
- **For example,** if you spend a lot of money on snacks maybe only carry a few dollars so your limited.

Who is an adult that could help you manage your budget?

How could they help you?

Step 7:
Reward

- To build great habits we need to reward ourselves when we do well. If you can follow your budget successfully for a month, **treat yourself!**

What is a way you could reward yourself for following your budget?

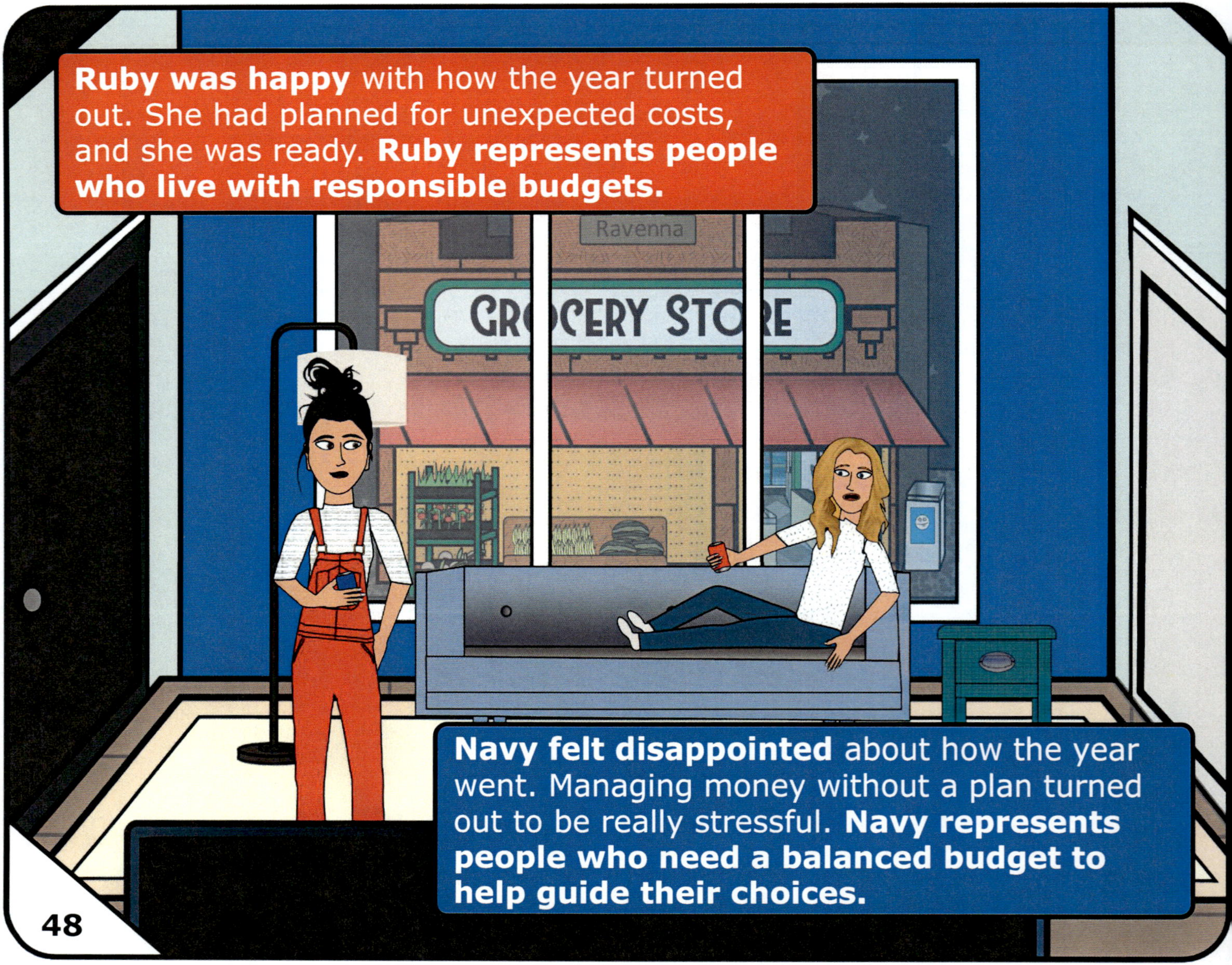
Ruby was happy with how the year turned out. She had planned for unexpected costs, and she was ready. **Ruby represents people who live with responsible budgets.**
Ravenna
Navy felt disappointed about how the year went. Managing money without a plan turned out to be really stressful. **Navy represents people who need a balanced budget to help guide their choices.**

What are your biggest takeaways from Ruby and Navy's story?

Ruby

Why was Ruby happy with her budget?

Navy

Why was Navy sad about her budget?

$150

Video Game: $50

New Hats: $30

Trading Cards: $30

Slime making kits: $25

Card Games : $15

When you take time to make responsible decisions everyone benefits. A budget might keep us from getting the things we want today, but they prepare us for what we might need tomorrow. Take a look back at your budget.

Was it more like Ruby or Navy?
Would you make any changes?

Step 2:
Observe how budgeting is a way to be financially responsible.

Beep-Beep-Beeeep! (Create your own story)

Come up with two characters and show how each one manages their money. What choices do they make? What are the results?

Write the story:

Illustrate the story:

I don't know about you, but limiting my spending can sound like a bummer!
But what if we changed how we see budgeting? If we treat it like a game, we can actually have fun and grow our money skills! Let's check out how you can gamified your spending with a budget!
BUDGET
BUDGET
DT-7G

To play any game, you first need to know what it's about.
Let's start with what makes a budget complete.

BUDGET

$

INCOME: Money earned for working.

EXPENSES

FIXED: Costs that are the same each month.

VARIABLE: Costs that change each month.

OCCASIONAL: Costs that don't happen monthly.

SAVINGS

GOALS: Money put away for things you want.

FUNDS: Money put away for unexpected costs.

INCOME

The money a person earns through work or investments.

As a teen, you can apply for a job and increase your spending power. As your skills level up, so can the ways you earn, and how much you get paid!

Babies depend on caretakers for money.

Children can earn money by doing chores.

Teens can get jobs to make their own money.

Adults have careers to earn income.

How can you level up in your income?

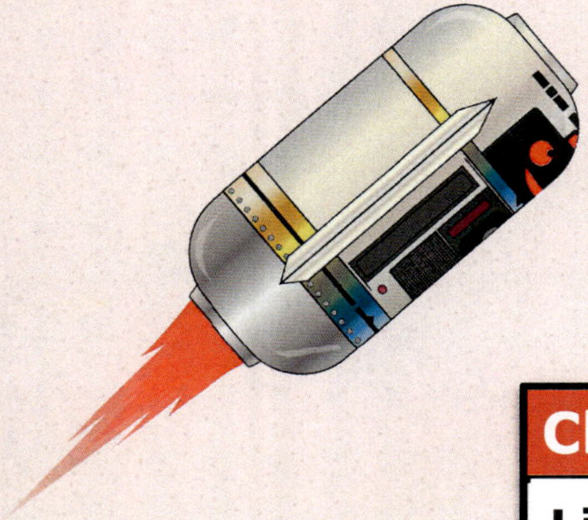

Baby

Babies don't earn money, they are completely dependent on their families.

Children

List 5 chores you can do at home:

Example:

Washing dishes

Teens

What are five types of jobs a teen could have? Include local examples.

Example:

House painting

Use Savings or Borrow

INCOME

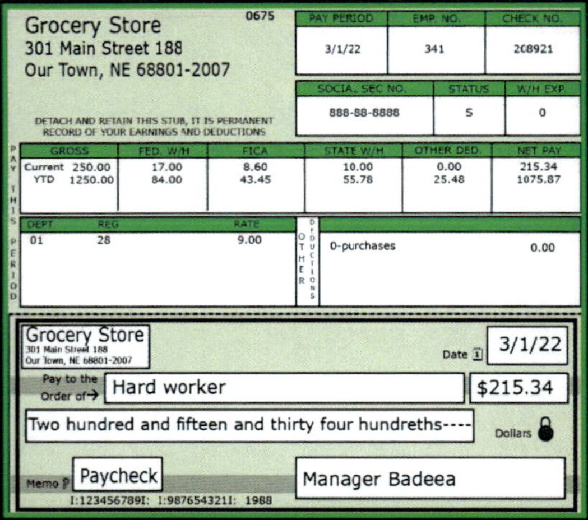

Grocery Store
301 Main Street 188
Our Town, NE 68801-2007

0675

PAY PERIOD	EMP. NO.	CHECK NO.
3/1/22	341	208921

SOCIAL SEC NO.	STATUS	W/H EXP
888-88-8888	S	0

DETACH AND RETAIN THIS STUB, IT IS PERMANENT RECORD OF YOUR EARNINGS AND DEDUCTIONS

PAY THIS PERIOD

	GROSS	FED. W/H	FICA	STATE W/H	OTHER DED.	NET PAY
Current	250.00	17.00	8.60	10.00	0.00	215.34
YTD	1250.00	84.00	43.45	55.78	25.48	1075.87

DEPT	REG	RATE
01	28	9.00

OTHER DEDUCTIONS: 0-purchases 0.00

Grocery Store
301 Main Street 188
Our Town, NE 68801-2007

Date 3/1/22

Pay to the Order of→ Hard worker $215.34

Two hundred and fifteen and thirty four hundredths---- Dollars

Memo Paycheck Manager Badeea

I:123456789I: I:987654321I: 1988

Your Income

Great habit: When you get paid, put some money into savings right away. It's one way to take care of your future self!

BUDGET

INCOME:	EXPENSES:	SAVINGS:
$3400	$0	$100 $1000

The first part of the game is earning money, because you can't budget money you don't have!

As you build your budget, your goal is to spend less than you earn.

If you spend more than you make, you might have to dip into savings or even go into debt.

EXPENESES

Life comes with costs, and this is where the game starts! To budget, you need to understand the different types of expenses.

Fixed Expenses:
(Locked In Expenses)
These are costs that stay the same each month in your budget.

Variable Expenses:
(In Control Expenses)
These are costs that change from month to month in your budget.

Occasional Expenses:
(Event Expenses)
These costs happen once in a while, not every month.

BUDGET

INCOME:	EXPENSES:	SAVINGS:
	$2100	$100
$3400	$2100	$1000

Time to get strategic! First is finding out what your costs are that stay the same each month. They are locked in!

Setting aside money for each of these recurring costs each month is an example of responsible decision-making.

Some examples are:

- Rent or Mortgage
- Car payments
- Insurance
- Streaming services

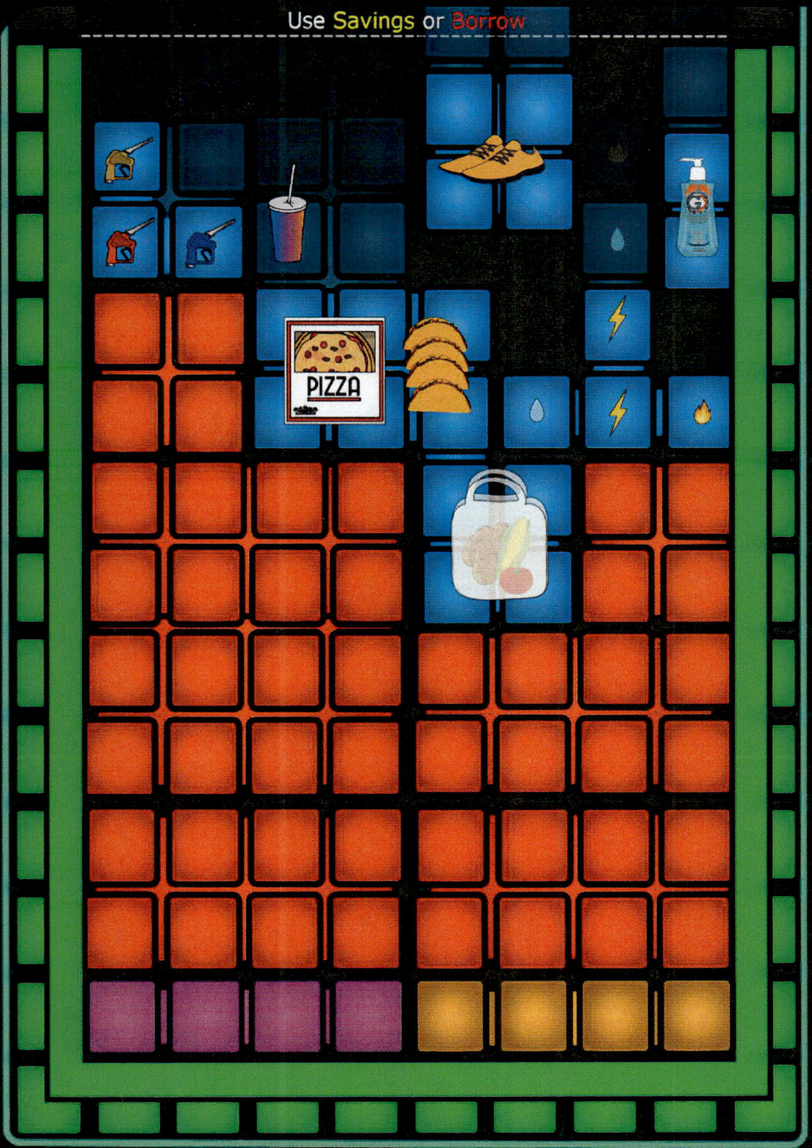

BUDGET

INCOME:	EXPENSES:	SAVINGS:
$3400	$800 $2900	$100 $1000

Next, we need to identify what costs you can control each month. You ultimately decide how much to spend on each of these expenses!

Set limits for these spending categories. This will allow you to spend money guilt-free! The power of a budget!

Some examples are:

- Groceries & Fast food
- Clothing
- Bills for your house
- Entertainment

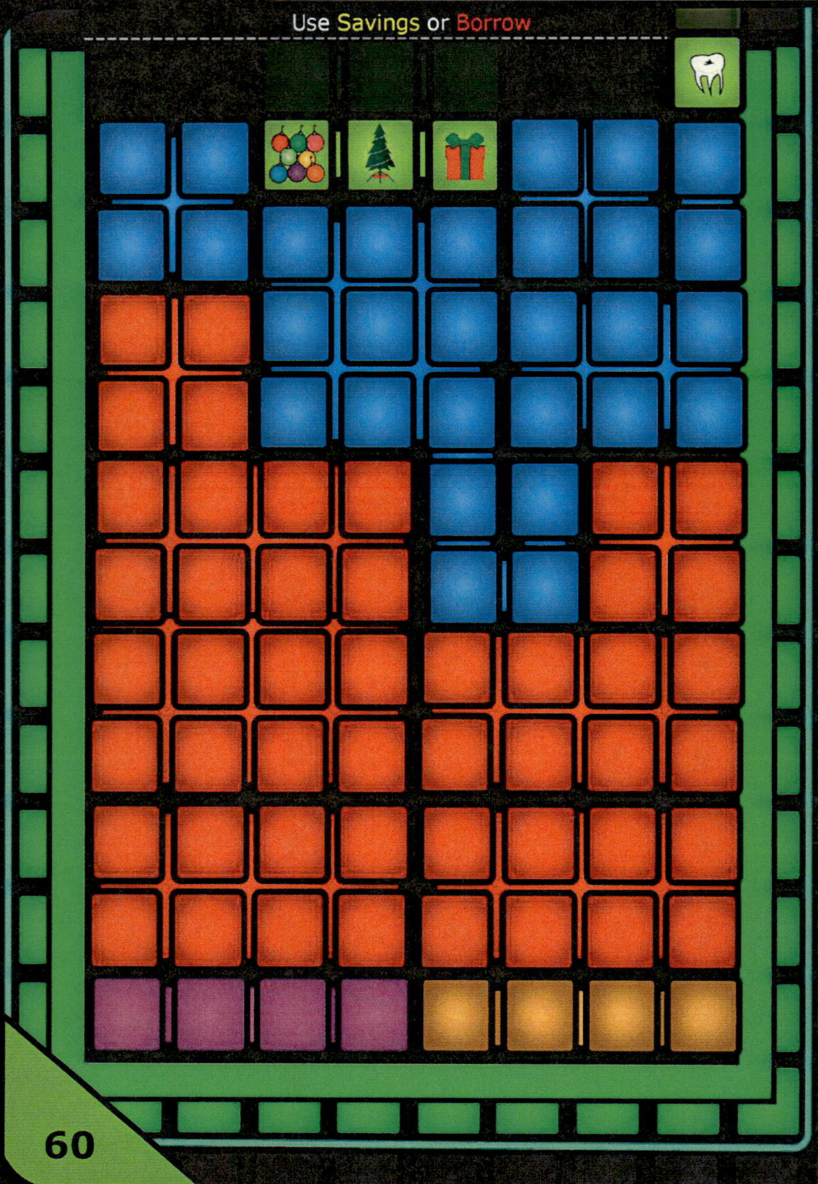

BUDGET

INCOME:	EXPENSES:	SAVINGS:
$3400	$3100	$1000

Life is full of special moments and you will want to think ahead about these events and prepare for their costs.

Having the money for these costs allows you to celebrate! Not having the money could lead to a lot of stress.

Some examples are:

- Holidays
- Appointments
- Trips
- Weather-related costs

Let's consider some of these costs?

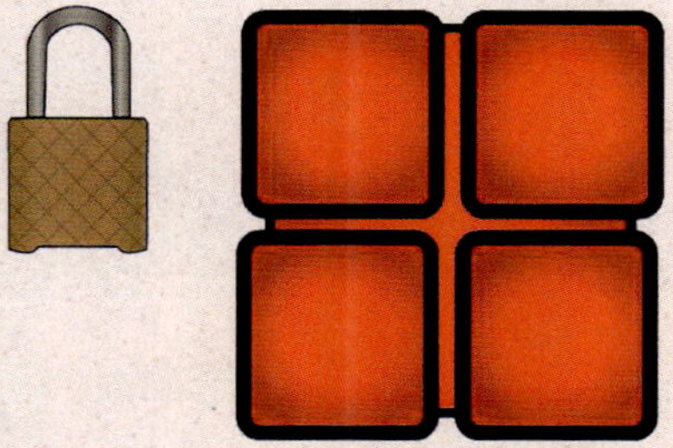

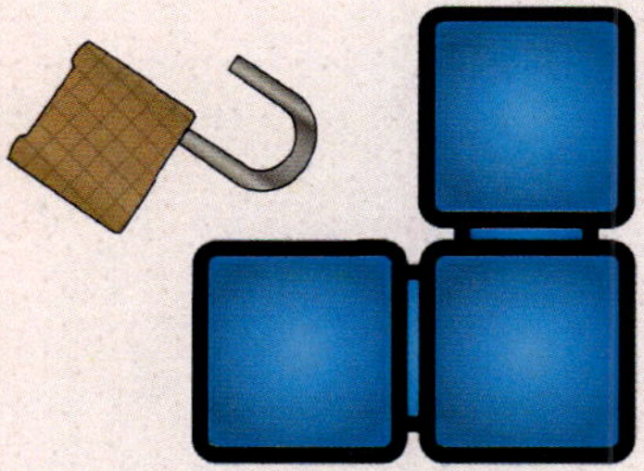

Fixed Expenses (Locked In)	Variable Expenses (In Control)	Occasional Costs (Events)
These costs are locked in, so it's important to plan ahead to cover them. **What is a subscription, and how does it work?**	These costs can change depending on how much you use something. **What's one expense you could cut back on if needed?**	Money spent on holidays can be planned ahead of time, while a trip to the dentist might be a surprise. **What holiday would you start saving for, and why?**

It's surprising how quickly expenses add up. Before you know it, you're left with just a few dollars. What's your next move?

SAVINGS

Money that is set aside for goals and possible future situations.

Here's a piece of advice: Don't spend all your money. It is important to have margin (space) in our budgets and our lives. **Spending everything creates financial stress.** This is just like staying up all night, which leads to feeling drained.

SAVINGS

Savings may seem boring, yet it can provide safety in scary moments. It can also give you funds for celebrating. **Savings teach us the power of delayed gratification, waiting for something better.**

Financial Goals:
Money that is strategically set aside for future purchases.

Emergency Funds:
Money set aside for urgent needs and emergencies.

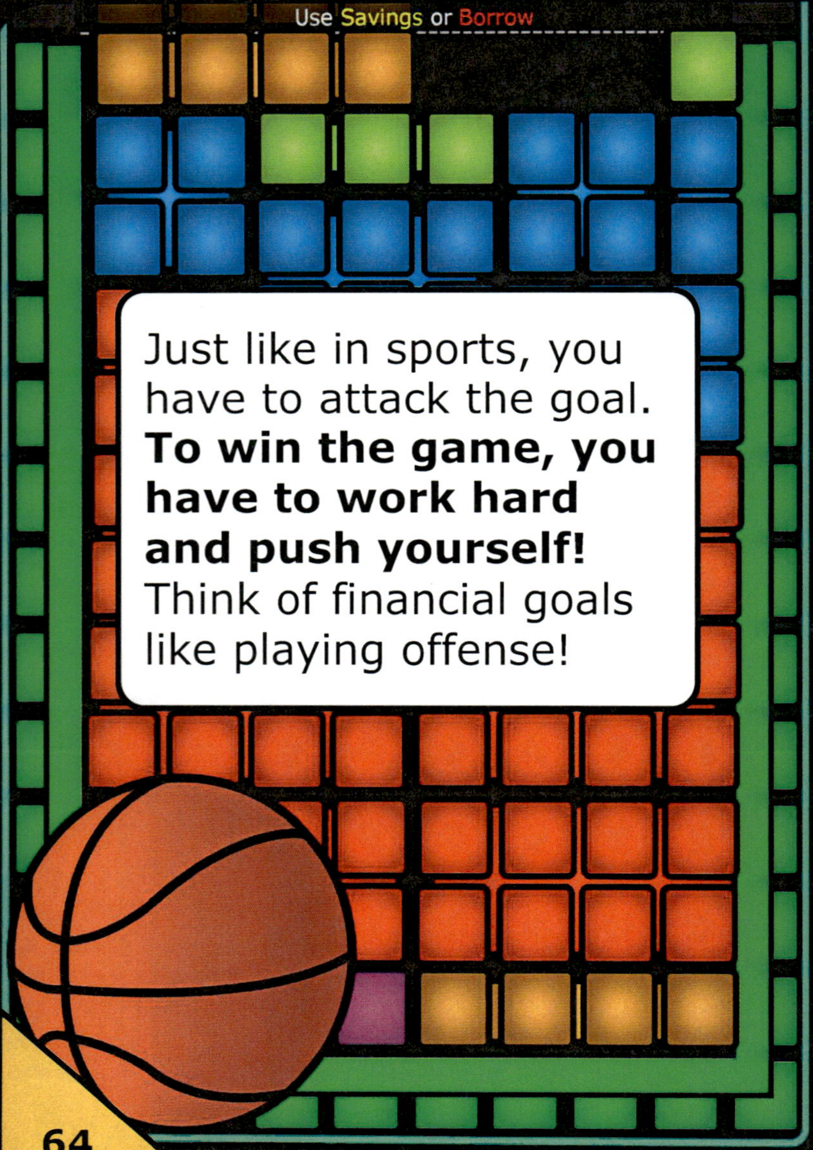

Just like in sports, you have to attack the goal. **To win the game, you have to work hard and push yourself!** Think of financial goals like playing offense!

BUDGET

INCOME:	EXPENSES:	SAVINGS:
$3400	$3100	$215 $1000

Savings comes at the beginning and end! On payday make sure to save. At the end of the money, take some that is left and save it!

Goals help give us the motivation to work hard and grow our skills. Start with a small goal and work your way up!

Some examples are:

- Vacation
- Saving for a vehicle
- Starting a business
- Retirement

Just like in sports, you also have to protect the goal. **To win the game, you have to consider threats.** Think of an emergency fund like playing defense.

BUDGET

INCOME:	EXPENSES:	SAVINGS:
$3400	$3100	$215 $1200

Be prepared! Savings help protect your future self from unexpected costs that could really hurt you! Emergency costs will happen!

Insurance is an important part of being responsible. It could be a little or a lot. That's why having money set aside matters!

Some examples include:

- Health issues
- Car repairs
- Home repairs
- Unexpected travel

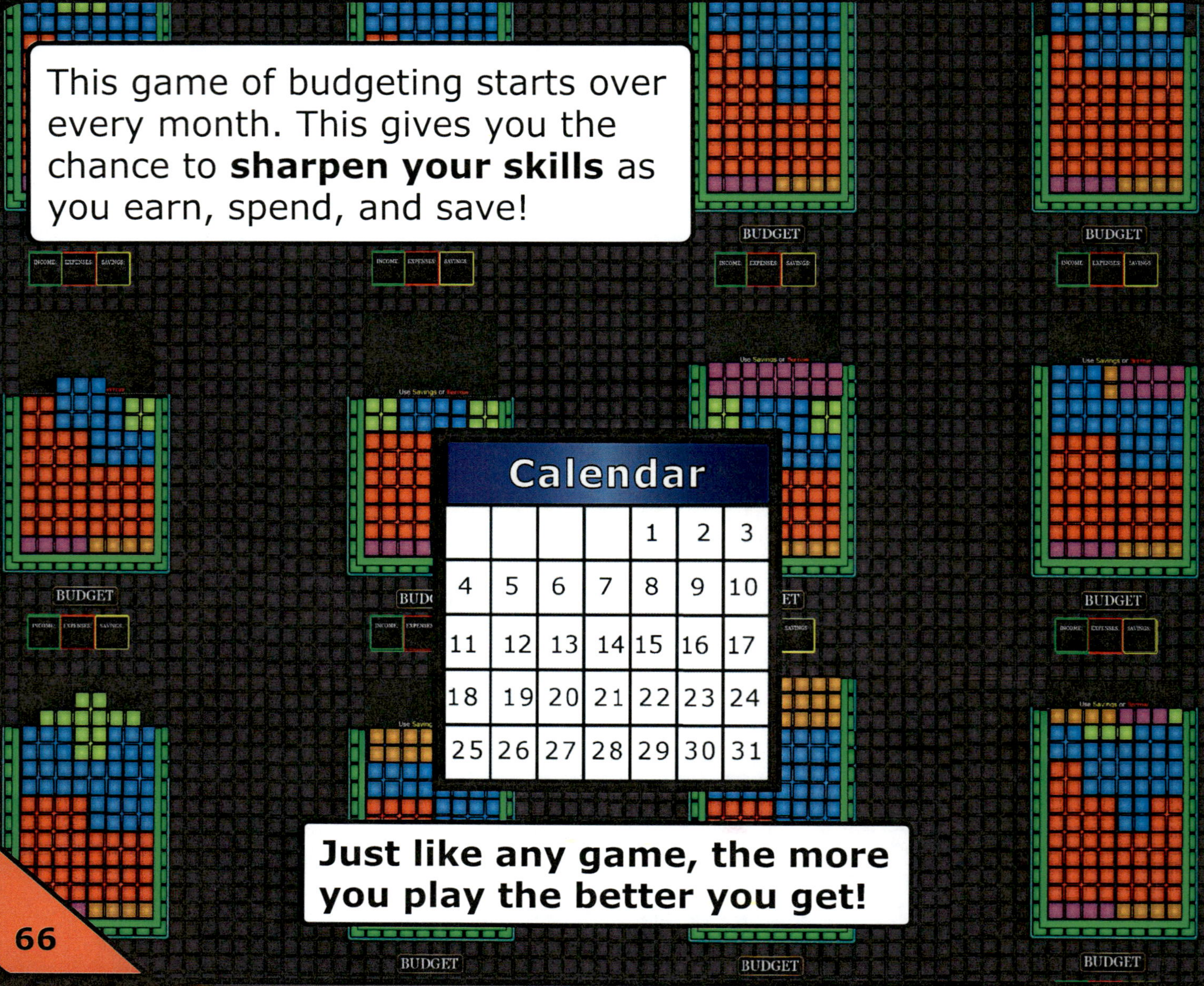

This game of budgeting starts over every month. This gives you the chance to **sharpen your skills** as you earn, spend, and save!

Calendar

				1	2	3
4	5	6	7	8	9	10
11	12	13	14	15	16	17
18	19	20	21	22	23	24
25	26	27	28	29	30	31

Just like any game, the more you play the better you get!

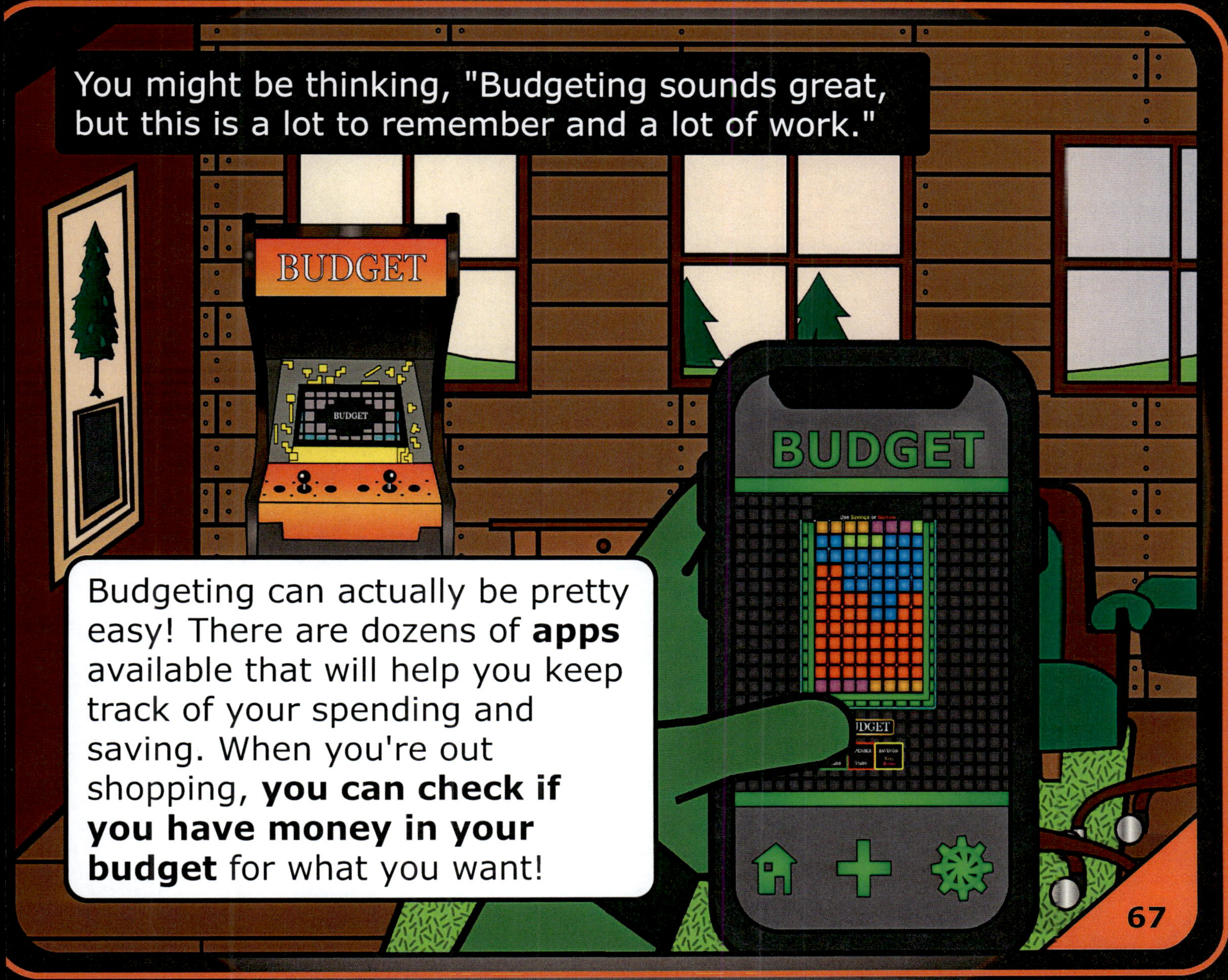
You might be thinking, "Budgeting sounds great, but this is a lot to remember and a lot of work."
BUDGET
BUDGET
BUDGET
Budgeting can actually be pretty easy! There are dozens of **apps** available that will help you keep track of your spending and saving. When you're out shopping, **you can check if you have money in your budget** for what you want!

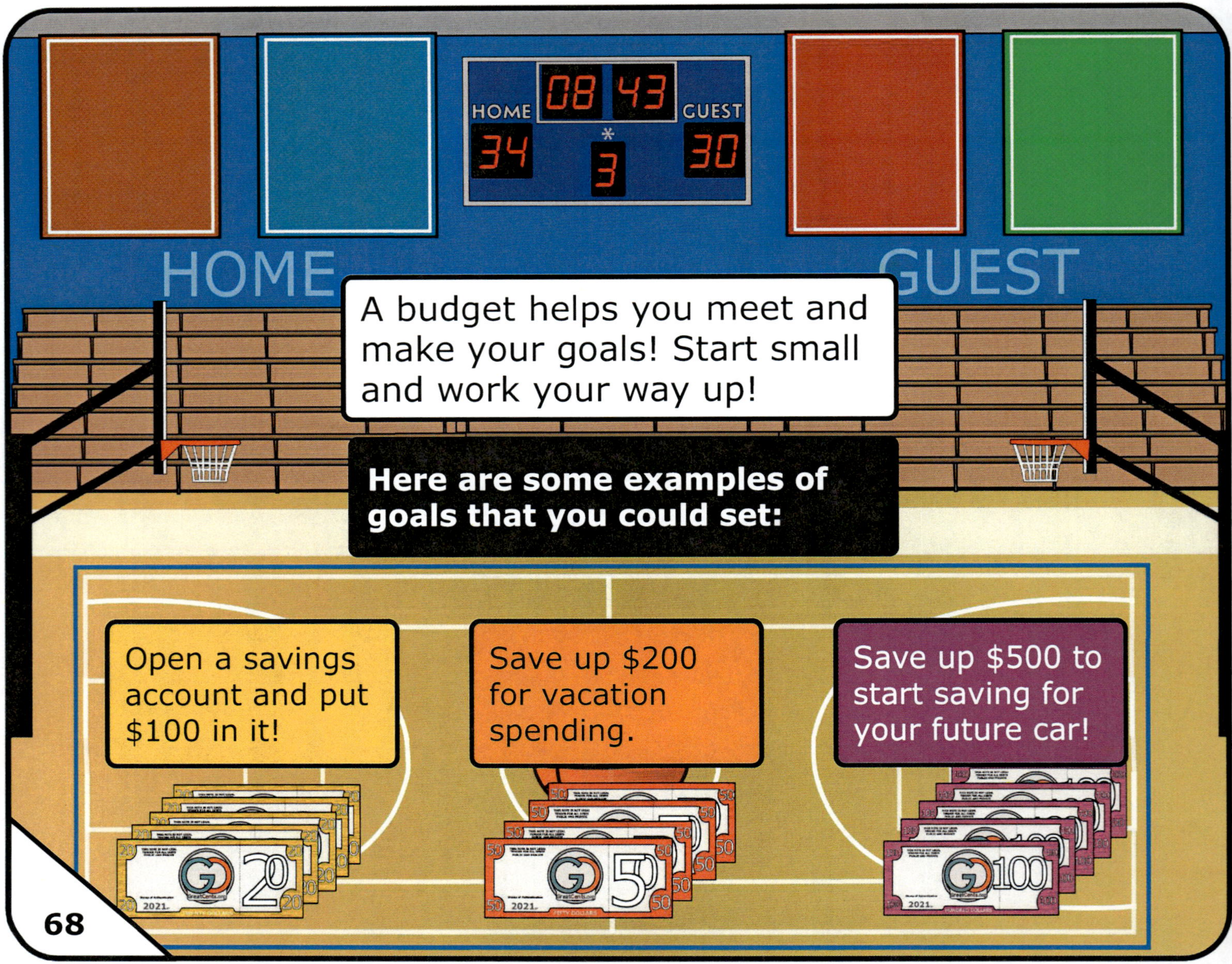

A budget helps you meet and make your goals! Start small and work your way up!

Here are some examples of goals that you could set:

Open a savings account and put $100 in it!

Save up $200 for vacation spending.

Save up $500 to start saving for your future car!

What are your stair step goals?

Goals Questions	Short term goal:	Medium term goal:	Long term goal:
What is something you would like to buy or do:	In three months?	In one year?	In three years?
How much will it cost?			
Saving!	How much could you save each week to reach your goal?	How much could you save each week/month to reach your goal?	How much could you save each week/month to reach your goal?
What can you do to earn or save that money?			

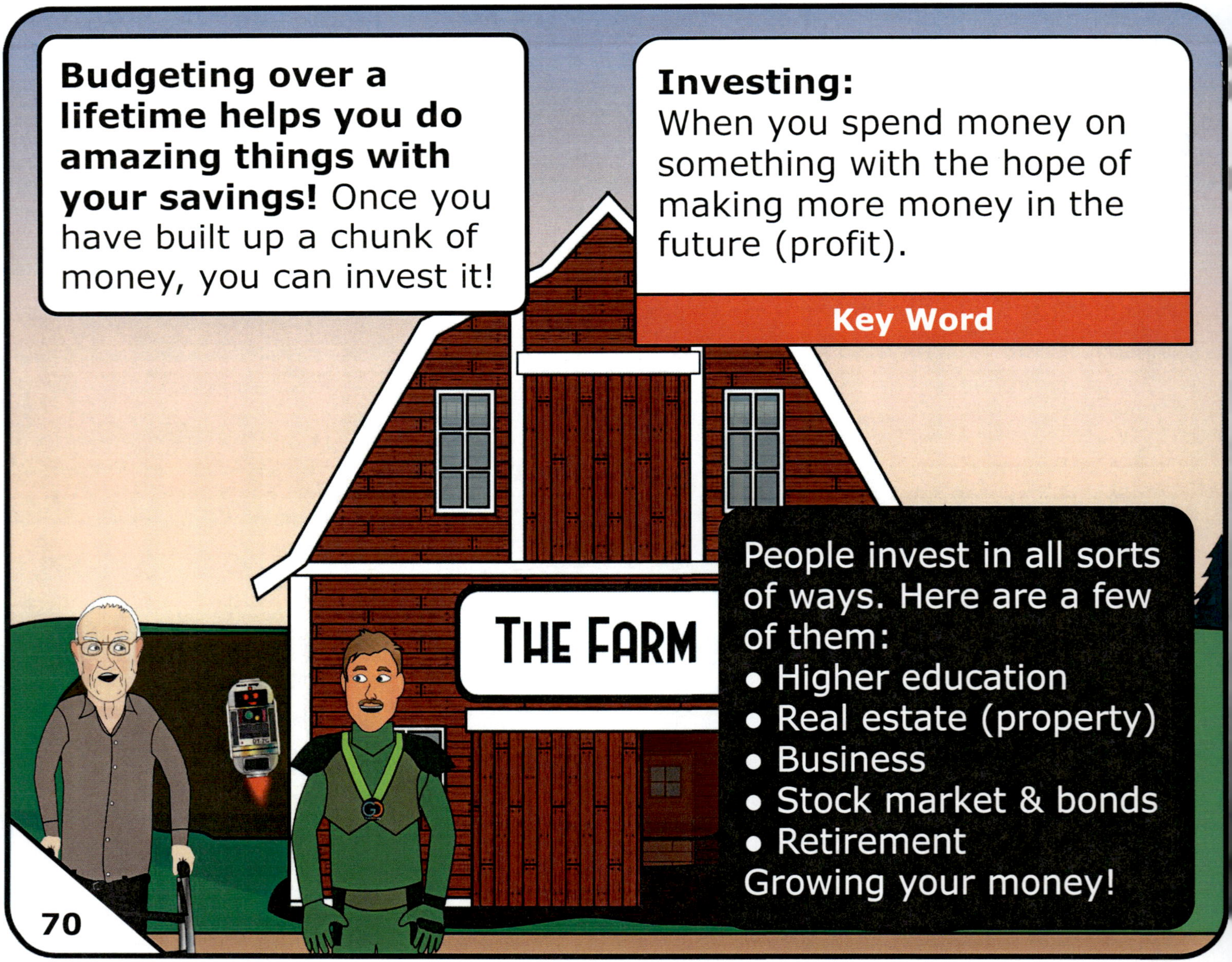

Budgeting over a lifetime helps you do amazing things with your savings! Once you have built up a chunk of money, you can invest it!
Investing:
When you spend money on something with the hope of making more money in the future (profit).
Key Word
THE FARM
People invest in all sorts of ways. Here are a few of them:
• Higher education
• Real estate (property)
• Business
• Stock market & bonds
• Retirement
Growing your money!

Just like a person needs to use a budget, so do businesses.

They buy supplies and pay employees.

EXPENSES

They save up in case of emergencies and hope to use money to improve or expand their business.

SAVINGS

They provide goods and services in order to make a profit.

INCOME

The same thing applies to governments and organizations.

Some people like to **donate** a portion of their savings to organizations they support. Organizations can serve your community (or even the world) in ways that we can't by ourselves.
Here are some examples:

- Health and helping people
- Environmental and animals
- Education and arts
- Religious and faith-based

Your money can help others help!

Donating:
When you give money to help an organization pay for its workers, programs, and advertising.

Key Word

Donating helps remind me that life is not just about me, but about others as well!

Step 3: Recognize the different parts of a budget and the power of saving.

Beep-Beep!

Describe each part of budgeting in your own words, and give two examples for each part.

Income	
Fixed Expenses	
Variable Expenses	
Occasional Expenses	
Financial Goals	
Emergency Fund	

Budgeting helps shape the way we live our lives. You'll start to see each day as 24 hours to budget. Build healthy habits into your schedule: sleep, exercise, healthy meals, learning, working, and socializing. Speaking of time, it looks like we've run out of it for today!

How do you budget your time? How would you spend your normal day?
Using the categories below write down what you usually do at that time.

Sleep	School	Eating	Friends & Family	Music/Sports	Shopping
Screen Time	Nature time	Chores	Travel	Other	

Midnight	1 AM	2 AM	3 AM	4 AM	5 AM
6 AM	7 AM	8 AM	9 AM	10 AM	11 AM
Noon	1 PM	2 PM	3 PM	4 PM	5 PM
6 PM	7 PM	8 PM	9 PM	10 PM	11 PM

Speaking of time, it looks like it's time for us to head out.
BUDGET
Z Z Z
DT-7G

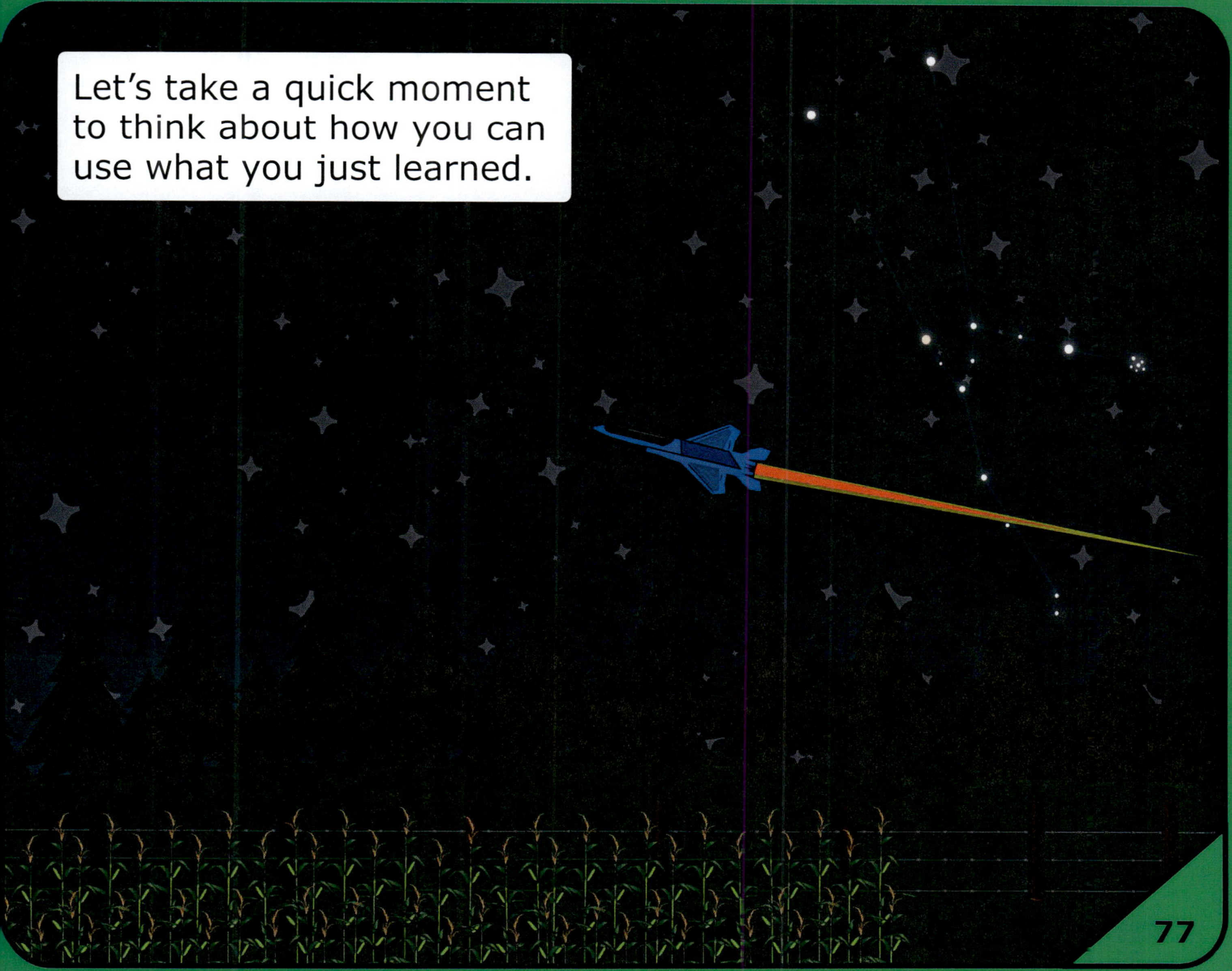
Let’s take a quick moment to think about how you can use what you just learned.

Pre-Teens

Let's see how a teen might experience the parts of a budget in their life.

Income	Allowance, chores, birthday or holiday gifts, and a job.
Fixed Expenses	Phone bill, subscriptions, and online memberships.
Variable Expenses	Entertainment, snacks, clothes, and transportation.
Occasional Expenses	Gifts for special events, vacations, and one-time opportunities.
Financial Goals	Gaming systems, vehicles, clothes, and donations.
Emergency Fund	Piggy bank or cash set aside for emergencies.

You

Income	Where do you get money?	
Fixed Expenses	What costs have you committed to?	
Variable Expenses	What costs can you control?	
Occasional Expenses	What special events do you spend money on?	
Financial Goals	What goals are you currently saving for?	
Emergency Fund	How much money should you have set aside just in case?	

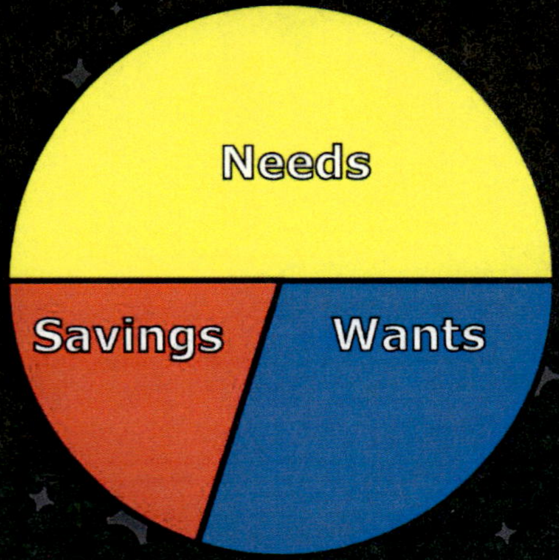

Needs	What are some of your needs?
Wants	What are some of your wants?
Savings	How much would you like to save?

You just got $200 for your birthday. How are you going to spend it?

Fixed Expenses	Variable Expenses	Occasional Expenses	Financial Goals	Emergency Fund
Subscription?	Snacks, clothes?	Events? Holidays?	Saving for goals?	Save just in case!
$	$	$	$	$

Add up your costs! Do they add up to $200? $

Adults

Now, let's see how an adult might budget. These are just examples:

Income	Job or career (wage, salary, or commission)
Fixed Expenses	Rent, car payment, insurance, internet, phone bill, and loans
Variable Expenses	Food, utility bills, clothing, entertainment, and repairs
Occasional Expenses	Holidays and celebrations, home renovation, and vacations
Financial Goals	Paying off debt, investing, saving for goals, donating, and retirement
Emergency Fund	$1,000 emergency fund, 3 months' earnings fund

Yourself at 25

Income	Where will you get money? What job or career will you pursue?	
Fixed Expenses	How nice of a house or car would you like to have?	
Variable Expenses	How often would you like to eat out each month?	
Occasional Expenses	What type of vacation would you like to take when you are twenty five?	
Financial Goals	How could you start investing at this age?	
Emergency Fund	What natural disaster could happen in your area?	

You have a job you really love, and you get paid $3,416 each month.

Spend it! Do the math and determine your costs!

Fixed Expenses — $3416

Rent $1456 | Utilities $420
Insurance $192 | Phone $99

$[ ]

Variable Expenses — $[ ] Left

Food [ ] | Clothing [ ]
Gas [ ] | Recreation [ ]

$[ ]

Occasional Expenses — $[ ] Left

Holidays/celebration [ ]
Big purchases [ ]

$[ ]

Financial Goals

Save [ ]

$[ ]

Emergency Fund

Save [ ]

$[ ]

What is the total? $[ ]

Thank you so much for joining us on this journey!
DT-7G

Let's look back at your journey. Did you meet your goals?

Step 1:
Identify the steps in making responsible decisions.

Step 2:
Observe how budgeting is a way to be financially responsible.

Step 3:
Recognize the different parts of a budget and the power of saving.

Step 4:
Create a budget for your current life and for the future.

Our Goal:
Make responsible decisions for our **personal** and **financial** lives.

Did we meet our goal? Why or why not?

Opportunity cost is the choice you pick. True or False?

True

False

What is the answer?

This expenses is one that you control?

Fixed

Variable

Occasional

Urgent

What is the answer?

Saving gives you the ability to give back through donating. What charity would you like to support?

Journal ...

In this lesson, you explored how **responsible decision-making** is key to organizing our lives, including choices about money, **budgeting**, and **saving for goals.**

How do you think growing in these areas could make your life better?

Build your budget!

On a piece of paper list:

- **Earning** - How are you earning money regularly?
- **Spending** - How do you want to spend your money?
- **Saving & Donating**- What is a goal you want to achieve? Where can you donate to?

Explore the Store!

Next time you're at The Store:

- Ask if you can budget $20
- Pick a budget plan to follow:

Example: 50-30-20

50% = $10 spend on needs
30% = $6 spend on wants
20% = $4 save for later

Mind & Money!

Planting seeds helps us to think about our actions today.

- **Pick a plant to grow.**
- **Grow it in a pot.**
- **Read the instructions and care for this plant as it grows. You are growing too!**

CentCity! (Bean Game)

You can find this game on our website or **TeacherPayTeacher**.

- You get 20¢ to pay for your different monthly expense.
- There are several versions where you can learn about inflation, the different ways of earning and taxes.

The journey of learning about our **Mind & Money** will continue!
Until we meet again, take care and spread kindness everywhere!

Opportunity cost is the choice you pick. True or False?

False

Opportunity cost is what you give up when you make a choice. For example, if you can have pancakes or toast for breakfast and you choose toast, then pancakes are your opportunity cost!

This expenses is one that you control?

Variable

Variable means something that can be changed, this means you have control over it.
Fixed means something that stays the same.

Saving gives you the ability to give back through donating. What charity would you like to support?

Answers will vary. There are many great charities making a difference in various ways. Students may want to explore local charities in their community or national organizations with larger missions. Giving helps us see the world beyond ourselves.

What's next?

You can continue the journey by joining us for the rest of the series. You rock for making your knowledge about **mind** & **money** a priority!

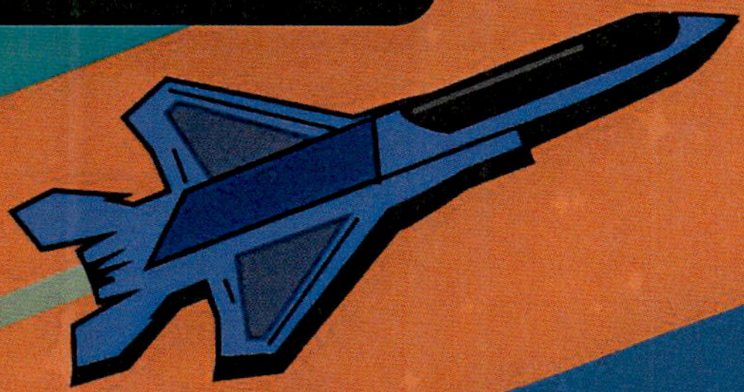

Glossary

Here you can find all of the major terms discussed in this book!

Budget	**37**	A plan for how you will earn, spend, save and donate your money.
Cause and Effect	**23**	When one thing happens (the cause), it leads to something else happening (the effect).
Donating	**72**	Giving money to help an organization pay for its workers, programs, and advertising.
Emergency Funds	**63**	Money set aside for urgent needs and emergencies.
Financial Goals	**63**	Money that is strategically set aside for future purchases.
Fixed Expenses	**57**	These are monthly costs that stay the same each month in your budget.
Income	**54**	The money a person earns through work or investments.
Investing	**70**	When you spend money on something with the hope of making more money in the future.
Occasional Expenses	**57**	These are costs that happen once in a while, not every month.
Opportunity Cost	**18**	What a person gives up when making a choice.
Perseverance	**45**	When you keep working, even when it gets tough, because you know it's worth it.
Priority	**10**	Something that is given higher importance.
Responsible Decision-Making	**9**	Recognizing the factors involved in making a choice and future consequences.
Saving	**84**	Strategically putting money aside for your future goals and emergencies.
Savings	**62**	Money that is set aside for goals and possible future situations.
Spending	**84**	The study of how you can budget money wisely and how prices are determined.
Variable Expenses	**57**	These are the costs that change from month to month in your budget.

Words are powerful!
They can open doors that
you would never imagine!

Check us out at
Teacher Pay Teachers

Our mission is to offer high-quality financial education resources for students at an affordable price. We invite you to explore our wide range of resources: lessons, games, foldables, and books. Thank you for your support!

- Cut along dotted line
- Fold
- Tape or staple

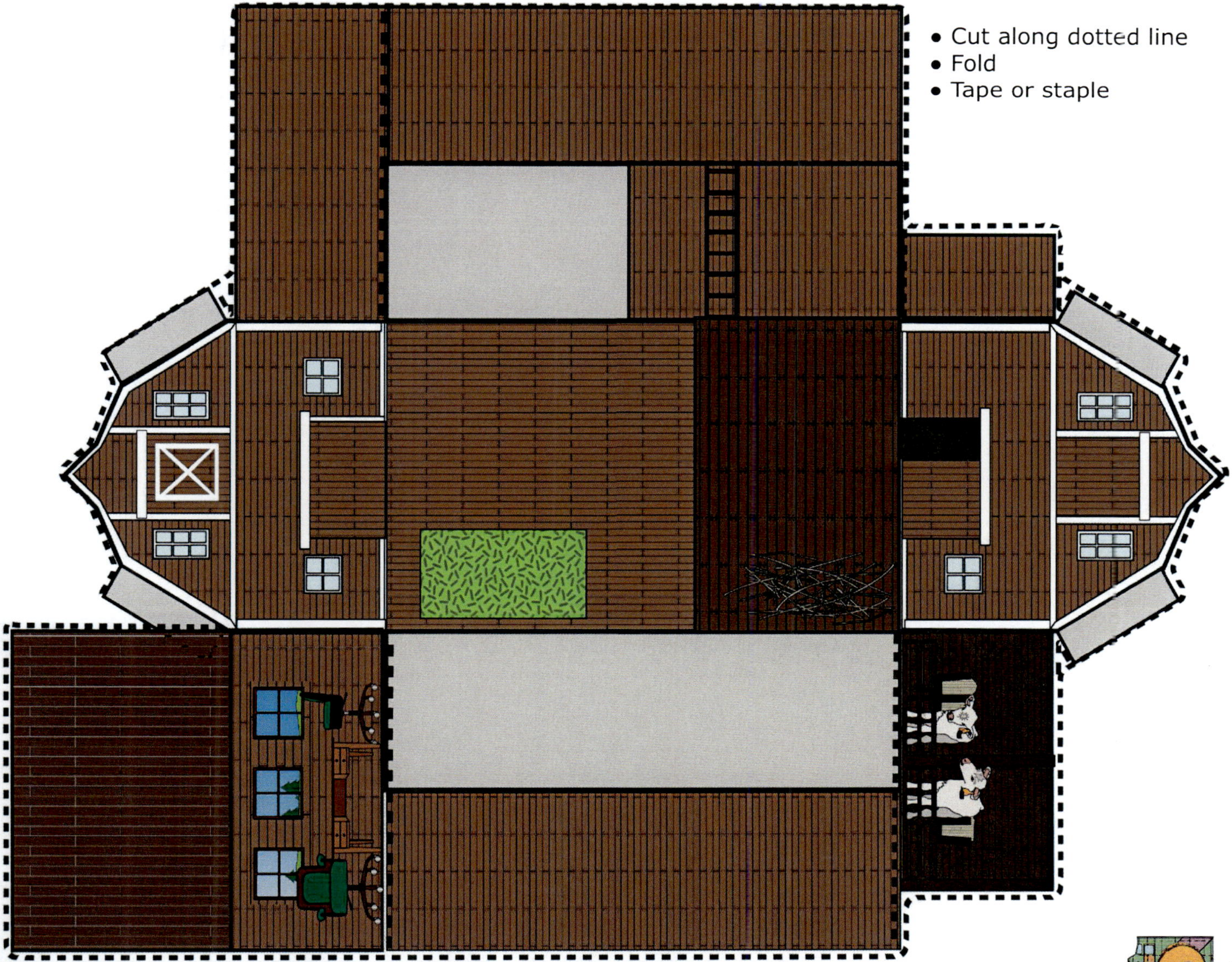

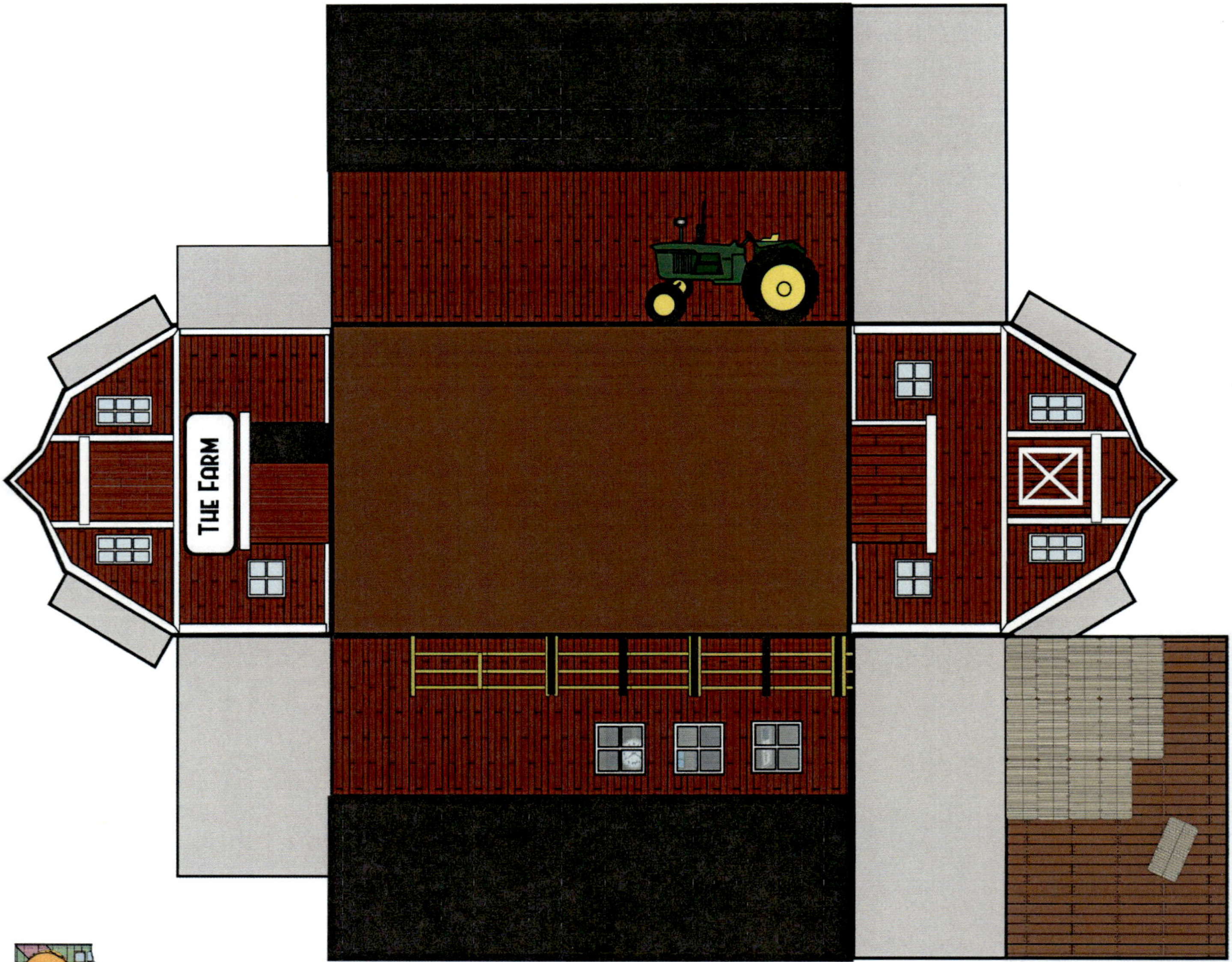
THE FARM

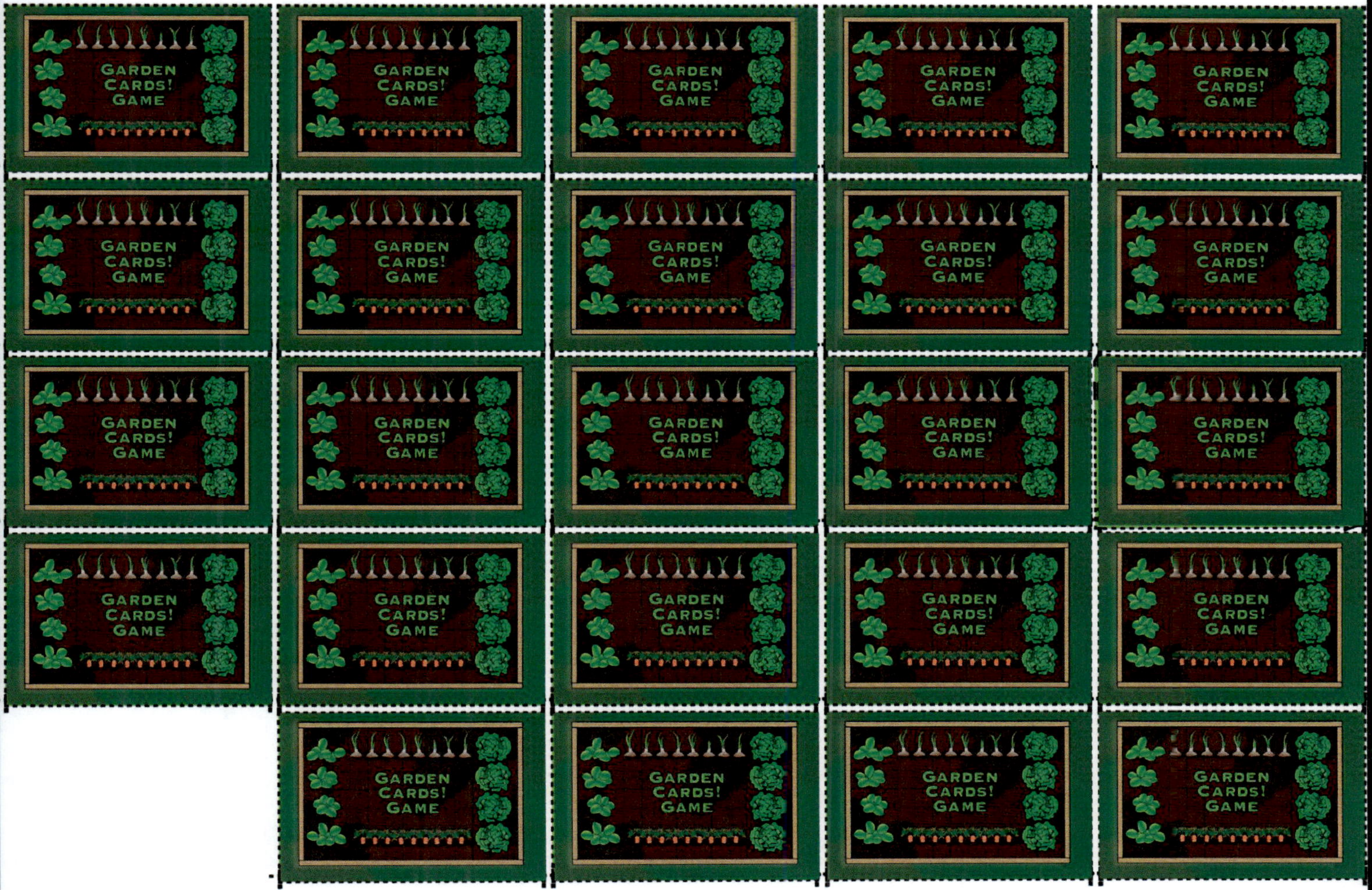
GARDEN
CARDS!
GAME

Garden Card Game!

How to Play: • Cut along dotted line • Place garden card side up • Flip over • Name the food • Each person share something that can be made with that ingredient • Repeat!